stories of

LITTLE
PEOPLE

in the BIBLE

used by a

BIG GOD *to*
IMPACT *their world*

WOODROW KROLL

BACK TO THE BIBLE

LITTLE PEOPLE BIG GOD
published by Back to the Bible
© 1998 by Woodrow Kroll

International Standard Book Number 0-8474-1472-8

Edited by Rachel Derowitsch
Cover Design by Design Resource

Unless otherwise noted, all Scripture is taken from *The New King James Version.*
Copyright © 1979, 1980, 1982, Thomas Nelson, Inc.
Used by permission.

For information:
BACK TO THE BIBLE
POST OFFICE BOX 82808
LINCOLN, NE 68501

1 2 3 4 5 6 7 8 9—04 03 02 01 00 99 98

Printed in the USA

Acknowledgements

In case you hadn't already noticed it, God uses little people to accomplish great things. These people aren't little in size, little in ability or little in strength. They are just people whose names are not household words. Many of the people whose stories are told in this book are not known to most Christians. Like little people today, they often worked in the background, in the shadows of obscurity. Yet, like those today, they were willing to be obedient to God and make sacrifices to serve him that others with the "big" names often would not consider.

I acknowledge that this book is the result of the effort of many such people. They are not little to me; they are giants. But you may not be familiar with their names and where better to acknowledge their large contribution than in a book about a big God and little people. I sincerely express my appreciation to Allen Bean, my researcher and assistant, who rewrote copy and made helpful additions; to Rachel Derowitsch, who contributed helpful corrections and editorial suggestions; to Blaine Smith, Director of Marketing at Back to the Bible, who was instrumental in guiding this project to completion and to Perry Boe for his cover design. I also am thankful to Bob Peterson and his team of professionals in our publishing department for their quality work in printing, cutting and binding each book. And to my secretary, Cathy Strate, who assisted me in cataloging, filing and scheduling the original radio messages which gave birth to this book.

Together it is our prayer that what follows will encourage all of you who make up the army of God's little people. Please realize that not only are you important to God, but you are vital to the work that He wants to accomplish in this world.

Rejoice with me. We have a big God who delights in using little people—people just like you and me.

LITTLE
PEOPLE
BIG GOD

Contents

Introduction 9

1. Jahaziel 13
2. Jabez 23
3. Eunice .33
4. Rufus 45
5. Hushai .55
6. Barzillai 63
7. Ittai 71
8. Ebed-Melech 81
9. Onesiphorus 95
10. Micaiah .105
11. Asahel .115
12. Jashobeam 125
13. Joanna .135
Conclusion 145

Introduction

We live in an era of superstars, men and women who have been pumped up by the media until they are bigger than life. With a wave of the hand they can draw crowds of tens of thousands and command unfathomable salaries for minimal output. It's hardly newsworthy anymore when, for example, Kevin Garnett of the Minnesota Timberwolves signs a contract extension for six years and more than $120 million, or Arnold Schwarzenegger gets paid $20 million for six weeks of work in his role as the bad guy in *Batman and Robin.* That's the world we live in, a world of superstars.

Unfortunately, the "superstar mentality" also has invaded the church. We have superstar pastors presiding over megachurches, superstar entertainers whose slick promotional material rivals that of their secular counterparts, and even superstar television personalities who are as concerned with their ratings as they are with their ministry.

It's refreshing to discover that God has no superstars. Certainly there are people like Abraham, David and Paul, who get a lot of attention in the Bible. They played very public roles in the development of God's kingdom. But they command no bigger "salaries" than the innumerable "little people" who are peppered throughout Scripture. People who are common, like you and me. People whose ministries can be summed up in only a few verses but whose impact will last for eternity.

In fact, when we get to heaven, we may be surprised as to who gets the top honors. Jesus gave a hint of that when He told His disciples, "So the last will be first, and the first last"

(Matt. 20:16). Someone who has a very public ministry with a great deal of praise from his contemporaries may find that a person who spent his or her lifetime secluded in prayer will receive far more rewards.

This book is concerned with the "little people" found in the Bible. Outside of God's Word, their names may appear only in Bible trivia games, but more important, they are written in the Lamb's Book of Life (Rev. 21:27). While they may not be known among men, they are known by God (John 10:3). And they have left a heritage that is of value today.

Join me as we walk among such little-known characters as Ebed-Melech, Jashobeam and Eunice. And reap the rich blessings found in their lives—the lives of little people, the lives of people like you and me.

JAHAZIEL

Name:	**Jahaziel**
Nationality:	Jew
Era:	Circa 855 B.C.
Location:	Jerusalem
Reference:	2 Chronicles 20:14-19

Most Memorable Accomplishment:

King Jehoshaphat was facing a serious disruption to the peace of his kingdom. The Moabites and Ammonites were teaming up with unspecified other nations to form a great army that was marching against Jerusalem. The situation looked hopeless. Jehoshaphat called for a fast, and the people stood together with their families to pray. Then suddenly, God brought a message of hope through a previously unknown spokesman—Jahaziel. His voice was strong; his message clear. "Do not be afraid nor dismayed because of this great multitude, for the battle is not yours, but God's" (2 Chron. 20:15). Single-handedly, this man was used of God to inspire the nation to battle—and victory.

CHAPTER 1

Jahaziel

The Battle Is Not Ours

Imagine sitting in a large audience waiting for a special event to begin. The lights are low and you are comfortable in the safety of your anonymity. You think you are just another dimly lit face in the crowd. Suddenly, a beam from an intensely bright spotlight pierces through the darkness, combs the crowd for a moment and then comes to rest on you. Not only is the spotlight on you, but so are all the eyes in the audience.

Perhaps now you know how Jahaziel felt on that day when the Spirit of God came upon him.

In the past, things hadn't been terribly quiet in Judah. The great king Jehoshaphat and his people had been continually involved in one military campaign after another. But finally Jehoshaphat returned to Jerusalem and was living in peace.

Unfortunately, it didn't last long. A storm was gathering across the Jordan River to Judah's east. The Moabites, Ammonites and another nation, probably the Edomites, decided they would push Judah into the sea. It was time for action again.

As a military commander, Jehoshaphat knew what his response should be. But as a man of God, he knew what he must do first. Second Chronicles 20:3 says, "And Jehoshaphat feared, and set himself to seek the Lord, and proclaimed a fast throughout all Judah." Verses 6-12 record the prayer of Judah's king in which he asks Jehovah to give them victory and judge their enemies.

Having a godly leader in a time of trouble is an asset for any nation. But having a godly populace is a helpful complement.

Judah had both. Jehoshaphat stood in the house of the Lord to pray and, we are told, "all Judah, with their little ones, their wives, and their children, stood before the LORD" (v. 13).

Families stood together before the Lord. It was a time of national threat, and it would take the family unit, together and lifting up the nation, to remove that threat. Families are always strengthened when they stand united—father, mother, children—all in obedience to God.

And Then It Happened!

Thousands were crowded around him. He stood with his family as a single face in a sea of faces. Then, as if a spotlight pierced through the darkness to shine on him alone, the Spirit of the Lord came into the midst of the congregation and empowered Jahaziel. Those around him did not feel the Spirit's presence or His power, but Jahaziel did.

Jahaziel was nobody special. Yet sometimes God uses the "nobodies," people just like you and me, to accomplish His will. Jahaziel was a Jew of the tribe of Levi. First Chronicles 20:14 tells us that he could trace his lineage back to the sons of Asaph, those whom David had appointed to minister musically in the temple. Yet this particular Jahaziel had never appeared in the Bible before, nor do we hear of him afterwards. He was just a face in the crowd, but on this special day God chose to communicate a message of comfort and encouragement to Judah through this unknown bystander.

Jahaziel's message, barely 100 words long, came directly from God. He said, "Listen, all you of Judah and you inhabitants of Jerusalem, and you, King Jehoshaphat! Thus says the LORD to you: 'Do not be afraid nor dismayed because of this great multitude, for the battle is not yours, but God's. Tomorrow go down against them. They will surely come up by the Ascent of Ziz, and you will find them at the end of the brook before the Wilderness of Jeruel. You will not need to fight in this battle. Position yourselves, stand still and see the salvation of the LORD, who is with you, O Judah and Jerusalem!' Do not fear or be dismayed; tomorrow go out against them, for the LORD is with you" (vv. 15-17).

What Jahaziel said was not just good advice; it was godly wisdom. He was a calming influence in a tense situation. He was a voice of faith in a time of testing. He was a spokesman for God, declaring how God's people should react when facing a seemingly hopeless situation.

Jahaziel's message has encouraged God's people down through the ages. If you want to watch God work in your life, if you want to see Him fight your battles for you and win, do what Jahaziel did as recorded in 2 Chronicles.

Clear Away the Clutter of Fear

Fear distorts our ability to see clearly, magnifying molehills into mountains. This stumbling block of Satan can even cause us to do foolish things, like disobey the Lord.

The Lord admonishes us, "Do not be afraid nor dismayed because of this great multitude." The expressions "fear not" and "be of good courage" occur in the Bible over and over. Apparently, we aren't the only people who live with shaky knees and jittery hands. Four times in the first chapter of Joshua, for example, God said to the son of Nun, "Be strong and of good courage" (v. 6); "Only be strong and very courageous" (v. 7); "Be strong and of good courage" (v. 9); and "Only be strong and of good courage" (v. 18). The message got through to Joshua, for soon Israel captured the impregnable fortress of Jericho.

In order to encourage young Timothy to battle Satan valiantly, Paul reminded his spiritual son, "For God has not given us a spirit of fear, but of power and of love and of a sound mind" (2 Tim. 1:7). Timothy needed to know that there is no place for timidity in spiritual warfare. You and I are also in conflict with the powers of darkness, and there's no place for us to be timid either.

It is God's design for a believer to live by faith, not fear. This doesn't mean we will never be afraid—of course we will. But we need not live faintheartedly when it comes to withstanding the

Devil or attacking his strongholds. Have faith in God.

Someone once said, "Fear knocked at the door. Faith answered, and there was no one there." Jahaziel's message was that God's people should not fear the number of troops massed against them. After all, the strength of our enemy is of little consequence when the omnipotent God is our Commander.

Conquering our daily battles with Satan begins by clearing away our fears. We need to respect our enemy—Satan is a more powerful being than we are—but we must never fear an enemy whom God has already vanquished. The Bible says, "Resist the devil and he will *flee* from you" (James 4:7, emphasis mine). That's not only good advice; it's God's Word. Whatever your facing today—a faltering marriage, cancer, loneliness, wayward children—reject your fears and embrace your faith. God is in control.

Recognize to Whom the Battle Belongs

Jahaziel also reminded the people, "For the battle is not yours, but God's." You may be all too keenly aware that Satan is at war with you. But ultimately he's at war with God. When the Devil lifted himself up in pride and made his five "I will" statements of rebellion against God, he did not say, "I will be like Tom, Dick or Harry." He said, "I will be like the Most High" (Isa. 14:14). Satan is already smarter than Tom, Dick and Harry combined. He doesn't want to be you or me; he wants to be God.

When Satan struggled with the Lord Jesus in the Garden of Gethsemane, and later on Calvary's cross, Christ was not Satan's target because He lived a sinless life. He was Satan's target because He is God. Satan's long war has been a war against God. We are soldiers in the Lord's army, but it's the Commander-in-Chief whom Satan truly wants.

It's important in our daily skirmishes with the Devil to remember what Jahaziel wanted Judah to remember: "The battle is not yours, but God's."

This truth runs throughout the Bible. When hostile tribes mounted a fierce attack on Nehemiah and his friends so that it appeared they would be unable to rebuild Jerusalem's wall, Nehemiah reminded the workers, "Our God will fight for us" (Neh. 4:20).

When the Assyrian king Sennacherib marched against King Hezekiah and the cities of Judah, the Jewish king reminded his people, "With him is an arm of flesh; but with us is the LORD our God, to help us and to fight our battles" (2 Chron. 32:8).

Joshua continually drove this message home to the Israelites, saying, "You have seen all that the LORD your God has done to all these nations because of you, for the LORD your God is He who has fought for you" (Josh. 23:3). And again, "One man of you shall chase a thousand, for the LORD your God is He who fights for you, as He has promised you" (v. 10). And on the day the sun stood still, Joshua reminded the Israelite army that their victory was not simply because of extended daylight but because "the LORD fought for Israel" (10:14).

At an earlier time Moses encouraged the Israelites concerning the enemies they would encounter in the Promised Land by saying, "You must not fear them, for the LORD your God Himself fights for you" (Deut. 3:22).

And do you remember why young David refused to arm himself with the implements of war when he faced Goliath? As he said to the giant, "Then all this assembly shall know that the LORD does not save with sword and spear; for the battle is the LORD's, and He will give you into our hands" (1 Sam. 17:47).

Keeping a cool head and a godly testimony under the pressure of the job is not easy. Struggling with financial pressures can be disheartening. But Jahaziel's message to Jehoshaphat and Judah is one we should remember each day. The battle is not ours but the LORD's. You'll be far more successful, and worry a lot less, if you remember who does the fighting for you.

Prepare to Fight Your Adversary

The rest of Jahaziel's story shows that God indeed did fight for Judah. But our once-in-a-lifetime prophet admonished God's people to be prepared to engage in battle nonetheless. God spoke through Jahaziel to muster the troops and give them their marching orders. Certain action steps had to be taken to be ready for battle. Relying on God to fight for them would never excuse Judah for not being primed to fight. Jahaziel challenged them, "Tomorrow go down against them. . . . Position your-selves."

Not only did they have to march to the battle site, but the armies of Judah also were commanded to take up battle positions. The Jews had to be ready to fight. They could not face their enemies from the comfort of their homes or the safety of their walled city. They had to leave Jerusalem and journey to the country of Ziz, where they would array themselves for battle. In other words, even if the battle belongs to the Lord, victory does not come to armchair spectators; it comes to willing warriors.

It's much the same with our battles today. Raising kids who honor the Lord is a battle. We cannot simply pray for them and hope for the best. We must set ourselves in battle array and assume battle positions. This means helping them establish a personal quiet time with the Lord every day. It means having a set time for family devotions and never violating that time. It means monitoring what they watch on television. It means attending church and Sunday school every Sunday and perhaps enrolling them in a Christian school. It means encouraging friendships that will build them up spiritually rather than drag them down. It means offering your home as a gathering place for their friends. The battle may be tough and long, but the victory is sweet and well worth the effort.

Let the Lord Fight for You

When the storm clouds gather and you have arrayed your-self for battle, perhaps the hardest thing in the world is to fight off the temptation to attack. After all, when you assume battle positions you expect to engage in battle. But when the battle is the Lord's, sometimes this isn't necessary. The Lord command-ed the people through Jahaziel, "Stand still and see the salvation of the Lord."

This was not the first time God's people were told to stand still and watch God work on their behalf. When the Israelites were fleeing from Pharaoh and their arduous Egyptian bondage, they came to the Red Sea. With Pharaoh's armies breathing down their necks from behind, and a wall of water in front, it appeared to be an impossible situation. But remember what Moses said to these desperate people. "Do not be afraid. Stand still, and see the salvation of the LORD, which He will accomplish for you today. . . . The LORD will fight for you, and you shall hold your peace" (Ex. 14:13-14).

God always wants us to take our battle stations and be prepared for battle; but after we have done that, sometimes He just wants us to stand still and watch Him work on our behalf. How much it pleases God to see us trust Him!

When our loving Heavenly Father said, "Be still, and know that I am God," He didn't mean to be still only in a quiet place of solitude. That verse continues, "I will be exalted among the nations, I will be exalted in the earth!" (Ps. 46:10). Sometimes we have to be still in the thick of the fighting, too, when it's hardest to trust Him. It is then that He can make it most clear that "the battle is the Lord's."

The Israelites heeded the words that the Lord spoke through Jahaziel. Jehoshaphat bowed his face to the ground. The Levites and others stood up to praise the Lord God of Israel. But they did more than that. They rose early in the morning and marched on the armies of Ammon, Moab and Edom. King Jehoshaphat shouted, "Hear me, O Judah and you inhabitants of Jerusalem: Believe in the LORD your God, and you shall be established; believe His prophets, and you shall prosper" (2 Chron. 20:20).

Judah praised the Lord and passed the ammunition (literally). Singers went before the army praising the Lord, and an ambush was set for the enemy. But then the strangest thing happened. The writer of 2 Chronicles records, "For the people of Ammon and Moab stood up against the inhabitants of Mount Seir to utterly kill and destroy them. And when they had made an end of the inhabitants of Seir, they helped to destroy one another. So when Judah came to a place overlooking the wilderness, they looked toward the multitude; and there were their dead bodies, fallen on the earth. No one had escaped" (20:23-24). God's people truly saw the salvation of the Lord.

Live Life God's Way

Living life without fear is not easy. We are all prone to be apprehensive about almost everything. To enjoy the abundant life that Christ intends for us, however, we have to live life God's way. That means we must clear away the clutter of fear. To give into fear is to admit that you don't trust God. Then you must recognize to whom the battle belongs. The battle is not yours, but God's. He is responsible for the ultimate victory. Be prepared to fight, but also be willing to step back and let God fight for you. If you are willing to commit your troops (family, friends, business, etc.) to the Commander-in-Chief, and if you are willing to fight for them against the attacks of Satan, you just may find the Lord saying, "Stand still and see the salvation of the Lord, who is with you" (v. 17).

Is there someone in your life who needs to hear a message of hope and encouragement? You can give them a book from a best-selling author. You can give an inspirational tape from a dynamic speaker. Or you can ask God to use you, even if for a few moments, to bring His message of hope to that person. Remember to tell him, "The battle belongs to the Lord."

Jahaziel had only a minute in God's spotlight. But he delivered God's message faithfully to the people. He was not a big-name Bible character, but that's the kind of people God uses—people just like you and me.

JABEZ

Name:	Jabez
Nationality:	Jew
Era:	Circa 1100 B.C.
Location:	Coastal Palestine
Reference:	1 Chronicles 4:9-10

Most Memorable Accomplishment:

The name "Jabez" is like a cool oasis in a dry desert. After naming 425 people without comment or commendation in a genealogy of the 12 tribes of Israel, the writer of 1 Chronicles mentions Jabez as being "more honorable than his brothers." Although he was born in sorrow and great pain, his life proved to be exemplary because he was a man of honor. His prayer demonstrates his integrity and his passion. His petitions were simple. He said to God, "Bless me"; "Enlarge me"; "Accompany me"; and "Keep me." He prayed to experience the fruit of God's blessings, to receive the fulfillment of God's promises and to actualize the power of God's presence. It is no wonder that this little-known saint received his request.

CHAPTER 2

Jabez

Man of Honor

Do you recognize any of these names: Shammua, Shaphat, Igal, Palti, Gaddiel, Gaddi, Ammiel, Sethur, Nahbi or Geuel? No? They're a pretty unimpressive bunch, aren't they?

How about the names Joshua and Caleb? Sure, these you know. Well, the ten men listed above were on the same reconnaissance mission as Joshua and Caleb, except they came back with the majority report and advised Moses not to allow the Israelites to enter the Promised Land, for there were "giants" there.

How about these names? Do you recognize Shammuah, Shobab, Nathan, Ibhar, Elishua, Nepheg, Japhia, Elishamma, Eliada or Eliphalet? Not too familiar? I would assume, however, you know their brother Solomon. These were all sons of King David born in Jerusalem. Yet none of them became king or distinguished himself in any way.

It is possible to pore through a long list of unimpressive names and have no reason to stop—that is, until someone in that list impresses God. Jabez was such a man.

The books of 1 and 2 Chronicles are written to record or "chronicle" the history of Israel. For the most part, the early chapters of 1 Chronicles are a dry and seemingly endless lists of names. In fact, by the time we reach 1 Chronicles 4:9, more than 425 people have been mentioned by name.

Then, suddenly and without explanation, there is a change. The brief biographical sketch given of Jabez in 1 Chronicles 4:9-10 is like a breath of fresh air in a stuffy room. It's an oasis in the midst of a dry and dusty desert.

Jabez left his mark amid a list of non-descript people. For what reason? What was there about this man that would cause the Spirit of God to stop and say, "I remember this man in particular; let Me tell you about him"?

Usually we remember people by some great accomplishment they have done, but no such achievement is recorded of Jabez. He was nobody special. He wasn't a priest or a Levite. He wasn't an athlete or a military hero. He wasn't even the son of someone important. Why, then, does he stand out in a genealogical wasteland?

Jabez is remembered not because of what he did, but because of what he was. He was honorable. The Spirit of God was so impressed with this man that He takes the time to camp at Jabez' name in the midst of his undistinguished contemporaries.

To gain a deeper understanding of why the Spirit of God calls Jabez "more honorable than his brothers," we must give attention both to his character and to his prayer, which resulted from his character. This information is contained in just two verses, 1 Chronicles 4:9-10. Let's sift these verses as a farmer would his grain.

The Character of Jabez

It's not often that so few words reveal so much about a man. In just two verses we learn more about the character of Jabez than we learn of others in whole chapters. We know that Jabez was both a man of sorrow and a man of prayer.

A man of sorrow

According to the Scriptures, "His mother called his name Jabez, saying, 'Because I bore him with sorrow.'" In Bible times names were very significant. The name "Jabez" means sorrow or pain. Some scholars have speculated that Jabez was born an illegitimate child and thus caused his mother emotional pain.

Notice that there is no mention of a father or a family name. The word *begot* does not occur in verses 9 and 10 as it does in so many of the following verses. If this is the case, Jabez is a Jewish lad without a father, an ancestry or an inheritance, and therefore he is an innocent source of shame.

But a more likely explanation is that Jabez was the child of a particularly difficult delivery. Perhaps his mother died just after the delivery. We have a similar story in 1 Samuel 4, where news came to Eli that the Ark of the Covenant was taken by the Philistines and his two sons had been killed in battle. Eli's daughter-in-law, upon hearing that her husband, Phinehas, was dead, abruptly gave birth in pain and with her dying breath named the child Ichabod, which means "The glory has departed from Israel" (1 Sam. 4:21).

Although "Jabez" means sorrow, his character soon proved that he was a joy to God. This should be a lesson to all of us. It's not how we begin the race but how we finish it that counts. You may have been born of humble parents; you may have had a slow start in life; you may have had to overcome some debilitating childhood disease. But how you began life's race is not nearly as important as how you run it and how you'll finish it. Don't let early defeats or failures keep you from a strong finish.

A man of prayer

Pioneer missionary Hudson Taylor once wanted to teach a spiritual lesson, so he filled a glass with water and placed it on the table in front of him. While he was casually speaking, he pounded his fist on the table, causing the water in the glass to splash out. He then explained to his listeners, "You will come up against much trouble and sorrow. But when you do, remember, only what's in you will spill out."

Jabez was a man of honor because what spilled out when he opened his mouth was a prayer. Jesus taught us that what's in a man will determine what comes out: "For out of the abundance of the heart his mouth speaks" (Luke 6:45). Jabez was right with God and when he spoke, his only recorded words were a prayer outstanding in both its brevity and beauty.

First Chronicles 4:10 notes that Jabez "called on the God of Israel." Herein lies the difference between Jabez and his brothers. He knew how to talk with God, and that alone made him more honorable than they.

These two qualities act reciprocally upon each other. Jabez was honorable because he was a man of prayer, and he was a man of prayer because he was honorable. That's true of us as well. When that which is on the inside is godly, that which spills out will be God-like as well.

As a man of prayer Jabez was a man of few words. His prayer is very short, yet remarkably comprehensive. Paul admonishes us, "In everything by prayer and supplication, with thanksgiving, let your requests be made known to God" (Phil. 4:6), and Jabez surely did that. Although his prayer is not long, it includes requests that are temporal, spiritual and eternal.

Someday when the books are opened, we'll discover that the more honorable people, as far as God is concerned, are the people who took the time to pray. Do your friends know you as a man or woman of prayer? It's important to be a person of service, but it's more important to be a person of prayer. Take time to pray, for when you do, you take time for God.

It is the character of Jabez that makes him notable in the chronicler's list of names, but it is the prayer of Jabez that makes him interesting.

The Prayer of Jabez

While the prayer of Jabez is short, it is 100 percent longer than any offered by the others named in this list. Yet its brevity contributes to its beauty. It is short, sweet and to the point.

There are four specific petitions to the prayer of Jabez. These are petitions for blessing, prosperity, presence and deliverance. They make an excellent guide for us when we pray.

"Bless me"

In Jabez' prayer, "Oh, that You would bless me indeed," there is no hint of a request for financial blessing. How uncommon that is. Perhaps Jabez knew that "the blessing of the LORD makes one rich" (Prov. 10:22). The blessing Jabez looked for was not on his purse but on his efforts.

God had promised His people an inheritance in the Promised Land, but they were unable to drive out the inhabitants on their own. Jabez, sensitive to his insufficiency, prayed that God would bless him in this struggle. If God would not bless him, Jabez knew that he would be as unsuccessful as his brethren had been.

How important it is that you and I estimate rightly the value of God's blessing. Jabez knew what James knew, that "every good gift and every perfect gift is from above, and comes down from the Father" (James 1:17). He was not praying selfishly. He simply wanted to get under the spout where God's blessing comes out. There's certainly nothing wrong with that.

But the blessing of God is not without purpose. We are blessed by God when we are in a right relationship with Jesus Christ and we ask Him to bless us. James says, "You do not have because you do not ask" (James 4:2). We ought to be hungry and eager for the blessing of God. "For you, O LORD, will bless the righteous; with favor You will surround him as with a shield" (Ps. 5:12). Jabez wasn't at all being selfish. He simply wanted what God had promised; others didn't. His prayer for blessing was legitimate, and one we ought to pray today.

"Enlarge me"

Even though this is a prayer for prosperity, it, too, is not a selfish prayer. Jabez' request to have his borders enlarged did not make him a land grabber or prosperity hunter. He was praying in the center of God's will. In Exodus 34:24 God promised, "I will cast out the nations before you and enlarge your borders." Deuteronomy 12:20 repeats, "When the LORD your God enlarges your border as He has promised you . . . ." There's nothing wrong with ambition as long as it arises out of God's will.

Someone has said the term *status quo* is Latin for "the mess we're in." Jabez was not content with the status quo. Israel had not conquered all the land that God promised them, and Jabez simply prayed that he would be faithful to the task when his less-honorable brethren had become weary and discouraged. That's not a bad prayer for us too. When so many have become diverted, so many discouraged in the work, so many disillusioned with their new life in Christ, let's pray that God will strengthen us and enlarge our borders. After all, the task the Lord gave us must be accomplished. If not by you, by whom?

The prayer for prosperity was not a "get-rich-quick" prayer, nor was it a prayer for God to make Jabez wealthy. It was a prayer of faith, a prayer of discontent with repeated failure. It was a prayer asking God to prosper Jabez' quest to fulfill the program of God. You and I should pray the same thing.

"Accompany me"

To the requests "bless me" and "enlarge my territory" Jabez added, "that your hand would be with me." The hand of God is a symbol of His strength and power. Ezekiel began his vision of the valley of dry bones by exclaiming, "The hand of the Lord came upon me" (Ezek. 37:1). When Nehemiah reflected upon why Artaxerxes, king of Persia, permitted him, a Jewish slave, to return to Jerusalem and rebuild the walls, he concluded, "And the king granted them [Nehemiah's requests] to me according to the good hand of my God upon me" (Neh. 2:8). To have God's hand upon your life is to have His power in your life. That's what Jabez wanted. It's what you and I should crave as well.

This little-known man of honor was not interested in going it alone. He knew if God's hand would not be upon him, he could never claim his promised inheritance. He prayed for God to be by his side and grant him the power of His presence. How could anyone fault that prayer?

It's not a bad idea for busy mothers, pressured businessmen, frazzled school teachers or anyone else to take some time each morning just to pray for the power of God's presence. We can have comfort for the long day when we know that we have God before us (Isa. 48:17), God behind us (Isa. 30:21), God on our right (Ps. 16:8), God on our left (Job 23:9), God above us

(Ps. 36:7), God's arms underneath us (Deut. 33:27) and His Holy Spirit within us (1 Cor. 3:16).

Like Jabez, we do not ask to be insulated from difficulty or danger; we simply want to be accompanied through that difficulty or danger by our faithful God. It's worth some time each day in prayer to assure that is the case.

"Keep me"

This is the prayer for deliverance from evil. The last clause of Jabez' prayer concludes, "and that You would keep me from evil, that I may not cause pain!"

This final petition of Jabez' prayer truly reveals his character. How reminiscent it is of what Jesus taught us to pray in the Lord's Prayer of Matthew 6:13: "Do not lead us into temptation, but deliver us from the evil one."

This is the most far-reaching entreaty of them all. Jabez requested God to preserve his honor, his purity, his usability. He asked God to guide his steps away from the source of evil, and to harness the evil one when he intrudes on his path.

What Jabez prayed may be considered a preventative prayer. Like preventative medicine, preventative prayer is something you do before you have a problem. If you're like I am, you need some time every morning alone with God to map out your day and ask Him to guide you through all the potential minefields that lay before you. Those things that are particularly trying to you need special preventative prayer. After all, we do not need to wait until we are in trouble to call on God. It's a better idea to call on Him to steer us away from trouble.

If you're not already in the habit of spending some precious time alone with God in prayer each day, you don't know what you're missing. Actually, those who do spend time with God may be the ones who don't know what they're missing. As the old hymn says, "Oh, what peace we often forfeit, oh, what needless pain we bear; all because we do not carry, everything to God in prayer."

Honorable Praying

Although the story of Jabez is contained in just two verses and we never hear from him again, there is a delightful postscript to his prayer. It is the notation, "So God granted him what he requested."

If we remember the magnitude of Jabez' request, we will have a greater appreciation for how God delights in answering the prayers of the righteous. God does not gain joy only by answering the big prayers of the Christian "superheroes"; He takes great delight in answering the big prayers of people just like you and me.

If we learn anything from Jabez it ought to be that the only thing necessary to stand out in a crowd is to stand up for God and call on Him in prayer. If we are truly men and women of honor, we are bound to interrupt the monotony of our genealogy and make a mark for God. If you want to leave a mark on this world, don't try to fit in. Try to please God, and He'll make your mark outstanding.

EUNICE

Name:	**Eunice**
Nationality:	Jew
Era:	Circa A.D. 50
Location:	Lystra, in central Asia Minor
Reference:	Acts 16:1-3; 2 Timothy 1:5; 3:14-15

Most Memorable Accomplishment:

The wife of a Greek unbeliever, Eunice was a faithful Jewess who loved God and raised her son to love Him too. From his early childhood she, along with her mother, Lois, taught young Timothy the Word of God. She did not shirk her responsibility simply because her husband was unable to fulfill his. Apparently she did an outstanding job, because when the apostle Paul came to Lystra looking for an associate to accompany him on his second missionary journey, he selected Timothy. At this choice Eunice remained silent. Even though it meant separation from him, Eunice had raised her son for the Lord, and now he was fulfilling his purpose. Eunice is an example for every godly wife and mother.

CHAPTER 3

Eunice

The Faithful Mother

One of life's greatest pleasures is a rainstorm. When an afternoon rain comes it means that Mom must find something for the kids to do indoors. Before television and VCRs invaded our lives, there was always a surefire way to entertain the kids on a rainy afternoon—the family photo album.

There are no laughs like the laughs of seeing yourself at a younger age—unless it's seeing Mom and Dad at a younger age. The family album is a great way to rehearse fond memories. It conjures up stories of the past that many adults have spent years trying to forget. Thumbing through the family album is just plain fun.

One of the neat things about the snapshots in a family album is that they show essentially the same people in their different roles in life. They give us insight into the many joyful relationships we have with our family.

In photo albums each of us appears larger than life. There are always pictures of Dad posing on the beach as a muscle man. There are snaps of Sis on her first date and Brother posed proudly with his first car (which now even he admits was a piece of junk). Then, of course, there is Mom. We see her in the kitchen on Thanksgiving Day. We see her fastening on boots so the kids can go out and play in the snow. We see her putting tinsel on the Christmas tree while Dad is busy struggling with something that came with instructions that said, "Some assembly required."

Snapshots from family albums teach us a great deal about our past as well as our future. They teach us about life and what's really important to us.

There is a mother in the New Testament whose family album I would love to have thumbed through. Her name is Eunice. She was the mother of Timothy, who was the understudy of Paul the apostle. Had there been cameras in those days, and if Timothy's family had kept a photo album, I think you'd find Eunice pictured in some wonderfully revealing ways. Let's peek into her imaginary photo album.

Snapshot One: The Believing Jewess

In recording Paul's second missionary journey (Acts 16-18), Luke reports that he came to the cities of Derbe and Lystra in Asia Minor, which today is Turkey. There he encountered a young man named Timothy, whom Paul had led to the Lord on his previous journey through that area. In order to identify which Timothy he was talking about, Luke says, "the son of a certain Jewish woman who believed" (Acts 16:1).

This "certain woman" remains nameless in Acts, but we know her name is Eunice from 2 Timothy 1:5. In this first snapshot she is pictured as a Jewess but one who believed on Jesus of Nazareth as her Messiah and Savior.

Synagogues were common in Asia Minor because a large number of Jews lived there. Eunice was Jewish because she was born of a Jewish mother. (One could be Jewish without having a Jewish father, but could not be Jewish without a Jewish mother.) Eunice, however, was a Jewess with an added dimension to her life—she was a believing Jewess. She had a right relationship with the God of Abraham because she had placed her faith in God's Son as Messiah and Savior. Today we would call her a messianic Jew or a completed Jew, one complete in Christ Jesus (Col. 2:9-10).

I'm glad this picture of Eunice is in the family album. After all, first and foremost is our relationship with God. Unless that relationship is correct, all the other photos of our life will be blurred and distorted.

Eunice was saved; she was born again; she was a Christian Jewess because she had placed her faith in Jesus' blood to cleanse her from sin. Faith has always been God's requirement for salvation from sin because "without faith it is impossible to please Him" (Heb. 11:6).

When the Lord told Abraham to look up to the manifold stars of heaven, promising that, though he was childless, his seed would be as the stars, Genesis 15:6 says, "And he believed in the LORD, and He accounted it to him for righteousness." Abraham believed God and was saved by faith.

As Jonah preached to the Ninevites, it is written, "So the people of Nineveh believed God" (Jonah 3:5). Faith brought salvation even to the most ruthless enemies God's chosen people ever faced. The Ninevites believed God and were saved by faith.

Psalm 78:22 tells us that the Lord's anger was kindled against His people because "they did not believe in God, and did not trust in his salvation." But when Israel believed God, when they trusted the promises of God to them, they were saved by faith.

Placing your faith in God's promise to save you is God's prerequisite to salvation. You don't have to clean up your life first; you don't have to become a Baptist, Methodist, Pentecostal or any other kind of church member. But you do have to believe on the Lord Jesus Christ as your only Savior from sin. Everyone who has been born again was saved by this same faith.

Jesus Himself said it this way: "For God so loved the world that He gave His only begotten Son, that whoever believes in Him should not perish but have everlasting life. For God did not send His Son into the world to condemn the world, but that the world through Him might be saved. He who believes in Him is not condemned; but he who does not believe is condemned already, because he has not believed in the name of the only begotten Son of God" (John 3:16-18).

Eunice trusted Jesus Christ as her Savior. Have you? If you're not sure, read the verses above again, be sincere when you tell God you repent of your sin, and believe that only Jesus can save you from the penalty of that sin. If you have never asked God to save you, do so now. He will.

Without question Eunice's most important relationship was her personal relationship with her Savior, Jesus Christ. It is the most important relationship any of us can have. Among her family photos, this snapshot must have been an 8" x 10" on the first page of the album.

Snapshot Two: The Delightful Daughter

I always enjoy seeing those mother-daughter pictures in my family album. My wife and I have three daughters and one son. With that ratio, we have a lot of mother-daughter pictures. Currently we have five granddaughters and one grandson. Again, there are lots of mother-daughter pictures in our family photo album.

The Bible tells us of very few mother-daughter relationships. There is the Syrophenician woman and her daughter, out of whom Jesus cast a demon (Mark 7:24-30). You may be familiar with Naomi and her daughter-in-law Ruth, who had been like a daughter to her (Ruth 1:16-17). But perhaps the best biblical snapshot of a mother-daughter relationship is that of Eunice and her mother, Lois.

In 2 Timothy, a letter Paul wrote to Eunice's son, the apostle gives us a tender glimpse of the family relationship between Eunice and Lois. He says, "I call to remembrance the genuine faith that is in you, which dwelt first in your grandmother Lois, and your mother Eunice, and I am persuaded is in you also" (2 Tim. 1:5).

Here is a hint of the unity between mother and daughter. Timothy's faith was a family faith, a faith first expressed by his grandmother and then by his mother. This does not mean that Timothy was saved by his grandmother's faith or his mother's faith. Each of us must have personal faith in Jesus Christ to save us; you can't get to heaven on your parents' faith. What it does mean is that both Grandma Lois and Mother Eunice instilled the principles of the faith in Timothy from the time that he was knee high to a hiccup.

Mother had instilled in daughter the need to trust God for salvation, and mother and daughter both instilled in Timothy an understanding of that need. This kind of family training is an ongoing process and should be evident in godly homes today.

One of the greatest delights of a Christian woman's life is the mother-daughter training program outlined in Titus 2:3-5. Perhaps when he wrote this passage Paul was thinking of Lois and Eunice. These verses read, "The older women likewise . . . admonish the young women to love their husbands, to love their children, to be discreet, chaste, homemakers, good, obedient to their own husbands, that the word of God may not be blasphemed."

It is both the privilege and the awesome responsibility of the older women of the church to teach the younger women the lessons they have learned through godly living. Some of these numerous lessons relate to taking seriously the responsibilities of being a godly mother, able to raise your children to be mannerly and God-fearing. Others pertain to how to love your husband, to submit to his authority and help him be a godly leader in the home. Yet other lessons involve being discreet, sexually pure and a good homemaker.

In our modern society, where most wives and mothers have been brainwashed to believe Satan's lie that being a homemaker is tantamount to being a slave, we could use some godly women around like Lois teaching some godly daughters like Eunice a thing or two about what God views as the high and extremely rewarding calling of motherhood.

There is a special relationship between a mother and her daughter. I remember when my first daughter was married. My wife, Linda, and our daughter Tracy spent months planning the wedding. That special teacher-learner relationship, which had always been there, reached its peak during those days. There was a bond formed between them that will last a lifetime.

Eunice was a delightful daughter to her mother. They must have shared everything, not the least of which was faith in Jesus Christ. And that sharing extended to Timothy. They shared with him the stories of God's deliverance of ancient Israel. They shared the more recent accounts of the apostles and the wonderful stories of how the Gospel was spreading like a fanned flame throughout the Roman world. But most of all, they shared with him Jesus.

Mother, you have the most privileged opportunity of anyone to share Christ with your children. Don't let the Sunday school teacher, the VBS worker or the AWANA leader be a substitute mother to your children. Share Christ with them yourself.

And Grandmother, when you rock those little grandchildren to sleep in your favorite rocking chair, don't waste your time with *Mother Goose* or *Grimm's Fairy Tales.* Tell your little ones about Jesus; sing songs to them about Jesus; help them come to love the One who loved them with His life.

Can't you almost see the photos of Lois and Eunice? Do you see young Timothy on grandma's knee? What scrolls do you suppose Eunice is reading from? Together they did whatever they could to raise him in the "nurture and admonition of the Lord" (Eph. 6:4, KJV). You can do the same with the precious gift God has given to you.

Snapshot Three: The Godly Wife

Look again at Timothy's family album. There's a whole page dedicated to his parents. There are pictures of Timothy and his dad fishing. There's one of his dad and mother kissing. And here's one of the three of them with their donkey. Grandmother Lois must have taken this picture.

Have you wondered why I've said nothing yet about Timothy's father? There's a good reason. Acts 16:1 tells us that Timothy's mother "was a Jewish woman who believed, but his father was Greek." There is a clear implication in this statement that Eunice's husband was not a believer in Christ. He was not a Jew nor was he a Christian. He was an unbeliever and a Greek.

This means that Timothy was born to a heathen and a Jew, from the Jewish perspective. It also means that he was born to an unbeliever and a believer, from the Christian perspective. We don't know if Eunice chose her husband or if her marriage was arranged by her parents. But if she fell in love with an unbelieving Greek and married him, then Eunice had forsaken the strong prohibition in the Old Testament about Jews marrying those from the nations around them. She had not followed God's will for the Jewish people. But in addition to that, she had forsaken the strong prohibition in the New Testament about believers marrying unbelievers (2 Cor. 6:14). Likely Paul had not yet written this when Eunice and her husband were married, but the strong restriction would have been implicit anyway. She had the double burden of an unequal yoke.

What could she do? She was a Christian wife married to a man who was not a Christian. What should she do? Being a godly wife, she did what the apostles taught and what the Scriptures command.

First, she did not lament her unhappy condition. She was in God's place for her, regardless of how she got there. A little verse says, "I cannot fill another's place; no more can she fill mine. God meant us each to fit His plan, not o'er our lots to pine." It was not God's perfect will for her, but Eunice was about to learn how to make something positive out of a negative circumstance of life.

Second, she did not seek a way out of her marriage because she was saved and her husband wasn't. Perhaps Paul had personally counseled her on her responsibility to her husband, counsel that he put in written form in 1 Corinthians 7:12-14. Regardless, there is no hint that Eunice ever left her husband or even thought about it. He was unsaved, but he was her husband. She would stay with him and try to win him to the Lord.

Third, Eunice lived a godly life before her unsaved husband. She became aware that she had a spiritual responsibility to him, and so she loved him and made her gentle spirit on the inside as glamorous to him as she made her hair and clothes on the outside. Maybe he would never yield his life to the Lord, but Eunice was determined that her nagging him would never be the cause of his failure to believe. She would do everything in her power to pray her husband to salvation, to witness to him discreetly and to live in a way that would attract him to the Savior.

If you are a Christian woman in Eunice's situation today, take heart. Eunice lived a complete life as a godly example to her husband. Read Peter's advice to women in your circumstance in 1 Peter 3:1-6. Keep praying for your husband, keep sweet before him, and keep the love of the Lord Jesus pouring out of your life. Remember, no cosmetic for the face can compare with the beauty of inner grace.

Snapshot Four: The Faithful Mother

I see a few photos in the family album of Eunice and Timothy alone. Some are when Timothy was just a toddler; others, when he was a teen. There is one photograph in which Eunice is hugging her son, as if she were bidding him good-bye.

These snapshots represent Eunice as a faithful mother. Although God has a plan for families—the father is to teach the things of God to his children (Deut. 6:4-9)—sometimes that just isn't possible. How could Timothy's father teach him about God when he didn't believe in God himself?

But this snapshot is very revealing. Just because her husband could not fulfill his role as a godly father, Eunice did not abandon her son to an ignorance of God or His Word. She jumped in to become both spiritual mother and spiritual father to young Timothy. I'm sure she appreciated Lois' help as well.

One of the best-loved verses in the New Testament is 2 Timothy 3:16: "All Scripture is given by inspiration of God, and is profitable for doctrine, for reproof, for correction, for instruction in righteousness." Just prior to this verse, however, Paul admonishes Timothy, "But as for you, continue in the things which you have learned and been assured of, knowing from whom you have learned them" (v. 14). Paul knew he would soon depart this life and he had invested a lot of time and energy in Timothy as a young understudy. Consequently, it sounds like he is lecturing Timothy to be faithful because he didn't want that time and energy to be wasted.

It sounds like it, but that's not what he's saying. When Paul says, "knowing from whom you have learned them," he is not referring to himself. Read the next verse. It says, "And that from childhood you have known the Holy Scriptures, which are able to make you wise for salvation through faith which is in Christ Jesus" (v. 15).

Paul didn't even know Timothy when he was a child. He couldn't possibly have taught him the Holy Scriptures. To whom could the apostle be referring? Without question, Paul was speaking of Eunice. She had been faithful in teaching young Timothy the Scriptures even though it was her husband's responsibility. Since Timothy's father could not fulfill that responsibility, Timothy's mother stepped in to be his spiritual mentor.

Abraham Lincoln said, "No man is poor who has had a godly mother." Behind Moses was Jochebed. Behind Samuel was Hannah. Behind John the Baptist was Elizabeth. And behind Timothy was Eunice. An old Spanish proverb says, "An ounce of mother is worth a ton of priest." I think Timothy had a ton of mother. He didn't need a priest.

Mothers, if your husband cannot fulfill his spiritual responsibility for one reason or another, don't abandon the spiritual training of your children. Take up the slack with love and wisdom. Remember, what you leave in your children is far more important than what you leave to them.

Snapshot Five: The Silent Servant

On the last page of the dusty photo album is a single picture. It's a bit wrinkled around the edges, as if it had been clutched to one's breast. There's a crack across one corner. There is even some evidence of a few dried tears on the surface of the photo. The picture is all by itself on that page. It must be something special.

What catches our eye immediately is that there is only one person in the picture—Eunice. She's all alone. Her mother isn't there. Her husband isn't there. Her son isn't there. She stands at the door of her little cottage all by herself.

Even though Eunice had taught Timothy the Scriptures since he was a child, she did not have the privilege of leading him to the Lord. That joy fell to Paul on his first missionary journey through Asia Minor. Timothy was Paul's own son in the faith. How Eunice must have thrilled the first time she saw Paul. The apostle was used of God to call Timothy to salvation. But the second time would be different. God used the apostle to call Timothy to service.

When Paul came to Derbe and Lystra the second time, he was looking for a young recruit to accompany him on his journey. Acts 16:2 indicates that the elders at Lystra and Iconium used their divine wisdom to discern that Timothy was the man. He had a good report in those churches, had served the youth group faithfully as president, was regular in church attendance and was an excellent witness for his Lord. Verse 3 indicates that Paul must have agreed because he "wanted to have him go on with him."

There were no ifs, ands or buts. Timothy was well qualified. Paul wanted him to go. The elders gave a rousing recommendation. What was left?

There stood Eunice. Deprived of a husband who knew the Lord, Eunice had only one godly man in her life—Timothy. Now Paul wanted him to leave her to serve the Lord on a foreign field. What would Eunice do?

Read Acts 16:1-3 for her response.

Don't find a response, do you? That's because it isn't there. She was a silent servant of the Lord God. Eunice recognized the truth of Solomon's statement, "Behold, children are a heritage of the LORD" (Ps. 127:3). She knew Timothy was not her possession; he belonged to God. God had only loaned him to her to raise. Timothy was a stewardship given to her by the Lord. She raised him for the Lord and she knew that someday He would want him back. She had prayed all his life that he would grow up to be a godly man, a useful servant of the Lord. Now that day had come.

Eunice's reaction to Paul's request was no reaction; her response was no response. When God calls our children, we should not manifest a sense of protection but a sense of pride. Eunice fully surrendered her son for service to the Lord. You and I must do the same! It's why God gave them to us. It's why He saved them. It's why He asked us to raise them to love and serve Him.

There is a greater sacrifice than the sacrifice of yourself to service. It is the sacrifice of your sons and daughters. Letting them go is always more difficult than going yourself. But service to the Lord isn't really sacrifice at all, is it? It's just humble submission. That's what faithful mothers do.

Memories

One lonely day Eunice probably found her old family photo album. For her this was more than just a trip down memory lane. It was an opportunity to see how God had led her through the good times and the bad times of life. Each snapshot represented a different role Eunice was called upon to play. Before God she was a believing Jewess. Before her mother she was a delightful daughter. Before her husband she was a godly wife. Before her son she was a faithful mother. And before the church she was a silent servant.

If I had to cast a vote for one of the outstanding women of all time, I may be tempted to vote for Mary, Jesus' mother, or for Amy Carmichael or for my own mother. But if that vote were cast on a rainy day in the attic, I think I would vote for Eunice, one of God's little people, a person just like you and me.

RUFUS

Name:	**Rufus**
Nationality:	Libyan
Era:	Circa A.D. 57
Location:	Rome
Reference:	Romans 16:13

Most Memorable Accomplishment:

When Paul wrote his greatest epistle, Romans, he sent greetings to the believers who were living at that time in Rome. He greeted 26 people by name in the final chapter. One of these is Rufus, whom he acknowledged as one "chosen in the Lord" (Rom. 16:13). That in itself is quite an endorsement, but the apostle also mentioned "his mother and mine." That the mother of Rufus, whose family originally came from Cyrene, was also referred to as the mother of Paul makes for an interesting interweaving of lives between lay people in the church and those called by God to work full-time for the Lord. In some way, Rufus shared a relationship with the apostle Paul that was more than just "brother in the Lord." Paul and Rufus had a unique family relationship as well.

CHAPTER 4

Rufus

Friend of the Apostle

"Elementary, my dear Watson."

You recognize that line. It's what Sherlock Holmes used to say to his sidekick, Dr. John Watson, when the great detective would deduce the undeducible.

What may have been elementary to the supersleuth, however, was always far less obvious to the rest of us. Yet given enough time and the painstaking process of piecing together the evidence, fragmentary as it was, we would always come to agree with the detective.

Romans 16 presents some mysteries that would be worthy of Sherlock Holmes. There are 26 people mentioned by name in this chapter, which implies that Paul had many friends living in Rome, even though he had not yet visited the capital of the empire when he penned this epistle.

Some of these friends are well known to us. Included are Priscilla and Aquila, coworkers with Paul in the tentmaking business, who had been vocal in their faith and had instructed many in the Word of God. And then there was Timothy, Paul's young protégé and traveling companion. We know a great deal about him. We know somewhat less about people like Jason and Sosipater, although they are familiar to us from other passages (Acts 17:5-9; 20:4). We know almost nothing about some (e.g., Andronicus, Urbanus, Tryphena and Tryphosa).

But who is the Rufus mentioned in verse 13? It's anybody's guess. What do we know about him? Very little. Are there any clues? A few, but if Mr. Holmes could solve his mysteries, maybe we can solve this one as well.

Let's go clue by clue and piece together the shreds of evidence that the New Testament gives about the life of this little-known saint. "Start us off, Dr. Watson, with an easy clue."

Clue #1

Our first clue to the identity of Rufus comes from his name. "Rufus" means "red" or "red-haired." Ordinarily we would assume that Rufus had red hair, but this may not be the case, especially given the subsequent clues we will gather. It's not impossible, of course, but it doesn't seem likely. If he did have red hair, that would make Rufus the New Testament version of Esau. When Esau was born the Bible says he "came out red . . . like a hairy garment" (Gen. 25:25). His name, too, meant red and he apparently did have red hair and a ruddy complexion.

Chances are, however, Rufus did not have red hair because he grew up in Africa. He was from Cyrene, an important city located 2,000 feet above the Mediterranean Sea and approximately ten miles inland. It was on a fertile plain where the climate was nearly ideal year-round.

Originally Cyrene was a Greek colony, founded 600 years before Christ. The Greeks had designs to make it the "Athens of Africa." This oasis in the desert attracted hoards of travelers and became a center of commerce. Consequently, there was a fairly large Jewish community in Cyrene.

A good detective's assistant like Dr. Watson would remember that Jews from Cyrene were present at the day of Pentecost. Included in the catalog of nationals on that occasion were those of "Phrygia and Pamphylia, Egypt and the parts of Libya adjoining Cyrene, visitors from Rome, both Jews and proselytes" (Acts 2:10). Watson also would help Holmes recall that when Stephen began his preaching ministry "there arose some from what is called the Synagogue of the Freedmen (Cyrenians, Alexandrians, and those from Cilicia and Asia), disputing with Stephen" (6:9).

There was a sufficient number of Jewish men in Cyrene, then, to have a synagogue (it took ten heads of families).

Perhaps commerce from Cyrene to the rest of the world took these Cyrenian Jews to Jerusalem and elsewhere.

Let's also not miss the fact that after the death of Stephen, the subsequent persecution drove believing Jews out of Jerusalem and across the Roman world. Acts 11:19-20 tells us, "Now those who were scattered after the persecution that arose over Stephen traveled as far as Phoenicia, Cyprus, and Antioch, preaching the word to no one but the Jews only. But some of them were men from Cyprus and Cyrene, who, when they had come to Antioch, spoke to the Hellenists, preaching the Lord Jesus."

Thus, not only was there a strong Jewish community in Cyrene, but there was a strong Christian community among the Jews there as well. In fact, this Christian community was so strong that some of the men of Cyrene traveled to Antioch to preach the Gospel. Could Rufus have been one of them?

"But wait, Sherlock. How do we know that Rufus grew up in Africa and was from Cyrene? You skated over that connection pretty quickly. What would make a good detective conjecture that Rufus was raised in Cyrene?"

"Elementary, my dear Watson. Follow my reasoning."

We know that when Jesus was crucified it was at the time of Passover. Thousands of Jews made the pilgrimage to Jerusalem at that time of year to celebrate. Mark 15 records the event of Jesus' crucifixion this way: "So Pilate . . . delivered Jesus, after he had scourged Him, to be crucified. Then the soldiers led Him away into the hall, called Praetorium, . . . and they clothed Him with purple; and they twisted a crown of thorns, put it on his head . . . . Then they struck Him on the head with a reed and spat on Him; . . . and when they had mocked Him, they . . . led Him out to crucify Him" (vv. 15-20).

Now here's where the plot thickens.

Mark continues, "Now they compelled a certain man, Simon a Cyrenian, the father of Alexander and Rufus, as he was coming out of the country and passing by, to bear His cross. And they brought Him to the place Golgotha, which is translated, Place of a Skull" (vv. 21-22).

Why would you identify a father by the names of his sons? Holmes reasons, "It must be because, while Simon was not well known, his sons had gained sufficient notoriety in the church to be recognizable to those who would read Mark's Gospel."

Holmes cannot be too dogmatic here. But if the Rufus of Mark 15 is the same Rufus of Romans 16 (it wasn't a common name; no one else mentioned in Scripture bears that name), then the detective can rightly make a connection between Rufus the man and Cyrene the city.

Piecing these clues together, then, it is likely that Rufus grew up in a Jewish Christian home in the Libyan city of Cyrene. His father may have been the man compelled to bear Jesus' cross on the Via Dolorosa. He had a brother, probably older, named Alexander. And, yes, he still may have had red hair; that we don't know.

"Watson, I think we've scored some major points with our first line of investigation. Let's go on to another clue."

Clue #2

"All right, Sherlock, what can you uncover about Rufus from the expression 'chosen in the Lord'?" Holmes will have to muster all his investigative reasoning here.

What does it mean to be a "chosen" servant? The original Greek word is *eklektos,* meaning "outstanding" or "selected." It's the same word Paul uses in Ephesians 1:4 when he says God "chose us in Him before the foundation of the world, that we should be holy and without blame before Him in love."

Does this mean that Rufus was chosen of God only in the sense that he was a Christian? No, it's more than that. If that were the case, why didn't Paul use this expression of Tryphena and Tryphosa in the preceding verse (Rom. 16:12)? Were they not also chosen in the Lord to salvation? Of course, but the apostle reserved the expression "chosen in the Lord" for Rufus and none other. Rufus was chosen in the Lord for something special. He was a choice servant, an outstanding servant.

What did Rufus do that distinguished him as such a choice servant? Not even the likes of Sherlock Holmes has a clue. The

Bible simply doesn't tell us. But we should not allow our lack of knowledge to dilute Paul's strong commendation of his friend and brother.

Once again we have the account of a simple servant of the Lord—someone just like you and me—who distinguished himself in the church at Rome by his outstanding service to the Lord. He wasn't a "supersaint"; he was just Rufus, a choice servant, a simple someone whom God used. He had all the qualifications you and I have, and maybe no additional skills or opportunities. But he used what he had to the glory of God.

"Okay, Holmes, but this second line of investigation did not yield as much information as the first."

"Then let's go on to the next clue, Watson."

Clue #3

Paul says, "Greet Rufus, chosen in the Lord, and his mother and mine" (Rom. 16:13).

"This is a stumper, Holmes. What possibly could Paul mean when he called Rufus' mother 'his mother and mine'? How was Rufus' mother also Paul's mother?"

"Elementary, my dear Watson."

Obviously this is not to be taken literally. If Rufus was from Cyrene on the north coast of Africa and Paul was from Cilicia in Asia Minor (Acts 21:39), they most likely would not have been biological brothers. Jews of Asia Minor would have been of lighter skin than Jews of North Africa. But this is where we must beware of brain cramps from thinking too hard.

Sherlock Holmes observes, "There's a clue missing, Watson. A piece of the puzzle has not yet been discovered."

Maybe we can assist the great criminologist. Let's go back to the historical record of Acts and retrace our steps.

After the persecution of Christians in Jerusalem, some fled north to Antioch in Syria. Remember what Luke observed: "Some of them were men from Cyprus and Cyrene, who, when they had come to Antioch, spoke to the Hellenists, preaching the Lord Jesus" (Acts 11:20).

When the Jerusalem church heard that a great evangelistic effort was underway in Antioch, they sent a representative to check it out. This representative was Barnabas, who, as soon as he saw how many people were being saved, departed immediately to Tarsus to find Saul. He knew these new converts needed to be taught in the Word and the task was too big for one man. Saul, now called Paul, was a master teacher and would be a huge asset to the church at Antioch.

This clue places the apostle Paul at Antioch while men from Cyprus and Cyrene were there ministering the Word. Could one of those Cyrenians have been Simon? Maybe. Could Rufus have been another? Might his family and he have fled from Jerusalem to Antioch after Jesus' crucifixion?

"Let's ponder that, Watson!" exclaims Sherlock.

But don't ponder too long, because just two chapters later in the historical record of the early church another important event occurs. Acts 13:1 says, "Now in the church that was at Antioch there were certain prophets and teachers: Barnabas, Simeon who was called Niger, Lucius of Cyrene, Manaen who had been brought up with Herod the tetrarch, and Saul."

Let's look at that list more closely. There was Barnabas, the apparent leader at this point. Then there was the man Manaen, who had been brought up with the tetrarch Herod. And interestingly there is a Cyrenian named Lucius. That leaves just the last two—Saul (Paul) and Simeon, called Niger.

It was a common practice in the New Testament era when dealing with men having the same name to add a nickname to tell them apart. For example, among the Lord's disciples there was Simon who was called Peter and Simon the Canaanite (Canaanean). There was also James the son of Zebedee and James the son of Alphaeus. Is it any wonder that the second Simon was called "the zealot" and the second James was called "the less" or "little James"? Think of how confusing it would be in a band of just 12 men to have two named Simon and two named James without some way to distinguish them.

Since Simon (sometimes spelled as Simeon) was such a common name, when Luke recorded the Acts he called the

Simeon of Acts 13:1 by a descriptive nickname—Niger. Niger simply means "dark-skinned." It does not necessarily mean black, but dark or darker than Jews would have been.

"Let's see, Watson. Libyans would be dark-skinned, darker than Jews but not as dark as Ethiopians. Could we make a connection between Simon Niger—Simon the dark- skinned—and Simon of Cyrene?" Perhaps so.

If Holmes correctly makes this identification, a lot of pieces fall into place in our puzzle. If Simon of Cyrene, father of Rufus, is Simeon the dark-skinned, that would place Simon and probably Rufus in Antioch at the same time Paul arrived there direct from his home in Tarsus.

"But wait a minute, Sherlock. That still doesn't explain how Rufus' mother could be Paul's mother!" Watson exclaims.

"Follow closely, Watson."

If Simon of Cyrene, who had darker skin, moved with his family to Antioch after the stoning of Stephen and became a worker in the church, that would mean he had a home established there. When Paul arrived in Antioch he was alone, with no family. The apostle needed a place to stay. Perhaps Simon took him into his house. Christians lodging with Christians was common in the first century (Acts 10:6; 16:15; 21:8).

If so, being alone in a strange town, staying with fellow believers and taking his meals there, Paul undoubtedly became a part of the family. Simon's wife, Rufus' mother, would have prepared meals, kept house and done laundry for Paul as well as Rufus and other siblings. In a very real way, she would have "mothered" Paul while he was a guest in their home.

Years later, when writing to the saints at Rome, Paul gleefully sent greetings to dozens of his friends including Rufus and, armed with fond memories of earlier days in Antioch, the apostle could not help but send greetings to "his mother and mine."

"It's all speculation, but there's a lesson to be learned here, Watson."

"Right you are, Holmes. Rufus and his parents teach us the lesson of Christian hospitality. You don't have to be a great detective to uncover that."

That's what people just like you and me need to learn from Rufus and his family. The writer of Hebrews begs us, "Do not forget to entertain strangers, for by so doing some have unwittingly entertained angels" (Heb. 13:2).

In our society today Christian hospitality has become a lost art. Families do not want to be put out when the visiting evangelist or Bible teacher comes to town. As a boy growing up in a pastor's home, I remember frequently sitting around the table with some great men and women of God. I learned as much from them at meal time as I did in church. Much of my own desire to serve the Lord was absorbed while sitting quietly and listening to story after story about God's marvelous work in the world. I wanted to be a part of that. If I had been sent away from the table or not encouraged to be present when visiting guests were entertained in my family's home, I would have had far less fertile ground for the Lord to plow.

I travel widely, and so I know that we have hotels and motels in most parts of the world that are convenient and not too expensive. It is now much easier to put a guest in one of them. And I know privacy is an important issue. I prepare many of my messages for the *Back to the Bible* broadcast while away from my study. I need that private, quiet time to study and prepare. But I always look forward to talking with preteens and teenagers in the homes where I stay. I have no hesitation to challenge them to think about a vocation in ministry. We need all the help we can get. When I stay in a motel, I don't have the same opportunity to influence young people for the cause of Christ.

So you're not a deacon or elder at your church. So you're not the Sunday school superintendent or even a Sunday school teacher. Does that mean you can't serve the Lord? If you have a clean home with a quiet, private room, offer it the next time a visiting preacher or a college singing group or anyone ministering for the Lord comes by. Can't do that? How about baking a nice dish to send to the house where they are staying?

God wants to use people like Rufus and his mother. He wants to use people just like you and me. But we have to become convinced that we are usable. Who knows? That young preacher still in Bible college whom you entertain may just be another apostle Paul. Someday he might even write to you, greeting you and his adopted "mom." Wouldn't that bring a tear of joy to your eye?

God's heroes aren't big people; they are just little people who make themselves available to God. Why not make yourself available to God in the same way that Rufus and his family did? Resurrect the art of Christian hospitality for a college student, a visiting Bible teacher, a traveling musical team. You know who will be the one who benefits most.

"Thanks, Sherlock, for helping us uncover another of God's heroes—people just like you and me."

HUSHAI

Name:	**Hushai**
Nationality:	Archite
Era:	Circa 979 B.C.
Location:	Jerusalem
Reference:	2 Samuel 15:32, 37; 16:16-18; 17:5-15; 2 Chronicles 27:33; Joshua 16:2, 7

Most Memorable Accomplishment:

Though he remained loyal to David and fled Jerusalem with him at the onset of Absalom's rebellion, Hushai soon found himself back in Jerusalem in his majesty's service. He acted as a double agent, giving counsel to Absalom but in reality giving the usurper son advice that was beneficial to David. Thus, this secret agent was able to thwart the evil scheme of Ahithophel, Absalom's chief counselor, and shorten Absalom's disastrous rebellion. With all the intrigue of a modern spy thriller, the story of Hushai is filled both with treachery and tenderness.

CHAPTER 5

Hushai

Secret Agent to the King

Everybody loves a good spy thriller. The essence of a best-selling spy story is the tug and pull between the good guys and the bad guys. Spy stories always include the chase, the double cross, the behind-the-scenes intrigue and maybe even trench coats and sunglasses.

Although it is highly unlikely that Hushai wore either a trench coat or sunglasses, his story has all the other elements of a best-seller. He was a counterspy for the king, and a good one at that. His story is riddled with excitement, but the bottom line is that Hushai was one of those little people whom God used to thwart the purpose of the enemy and save the life of the king.

Let's set the scene for the story of this secret agent to the king.

Have you ever noticed that some wounds hurt more deeply than others? When we are betrayed by a friend, it causes heartache; when we are betrayed by a loved one, it causes heartbreak.

David was betrayed by his own son. It is obvious that Absalom was one of David's favorite sons. When Absalom took refuge for his life, hiding out with the king of Geshur for three long years, it is said that "David mourned for his son every day" (2 Sam. 13:37). Apparently Absalom was a strikingly handsome man. Second Samuel 14:25 reports, "Now in all Israel there was no one praised as much as Absalom for his good looks. From the sole of his foot to the crown of his head there was no blemish in him."

Handsome or not, Absalom's career was erratic at best. At one point, he lived two full years in Jerusalem without seeing his father's face. This hurt him deeply, so the first chance he got, Absalom attempted to steal the hearts of Israel away from his father, King David. And he was very successful. The son usurped the throne and wrested the kingdom away from David, who had to flee Jerusalem, cross the Jordan and hide in the mountains beyond the river.

In this atmosphere of revolution, mystery and intrigue, we discover the story of one of God's little people—Hushai, secret agent to the king.

The Plan

When David escaped from Jerusalem, an entire entourage fled with him. They assembled at the palace, curled around the Hill of Ophel, and then crossed down through the Valley Kidron to the Mount of Olives on the east side of Jerusalem. From there David and company ascended the mountains and charted their course of escape through the wilderness to the Jordan Valley. When the deposed king reached the top of the mountain, he paused to worship God. What a perfect spot, overlooking the capital city of Israel, God's city—Jerusalem. Still, the circumstances were disheartening. David had just learned that a trusted advisor, Ahithophel, had joined Absalom's conspiracy and would not be fleeing with him. This must have been a crushing blow to David. Ahithophel knew David's cause was just, but often the lure of power is stronger than the commitment to justice.

Suddenly another of David's advisors approached him. It was Hushai the Archite. He had torn his garments and sprinkled dirt on his head, an ancient Near Eastern custom to demonstrate severe anguish and mourning. Hushai had chosen to remain true to God's king. He was willing to flee with David and suffer the hardships of exile rather than sell out to convenience.

But it was not to be. David cherished Hushai's allegiance, but the king hatched a plan that would make better use of his loyalty. Hushai would become David's spy in Absalom's court.

He was sent back to the new king to say that as he had been the servant of the father, now he would be the servant of the son. As a spy in King Absalom's court, Hushai could counter the influence of Ahithophel.

The plan was brilliant. Hushai was the inside man. He would gather intelligence from right under Absalom's nose and dispatch it to David. That way the deposed king would know every move his son made. As was the case in the world wars, the Persian Gulf War and most other conflicts, dependable intelligence would be the key to victory.

The Operatives

Every good intelligence-gathering operation needs more than one player to make it successful. More than one person would be needed to insure that Ahithophel's counsel would be countermanded. So who are the other operatives in this story?

First, there is Hushai himself. He's the spy, the mole in Absalom's court. He gathered the information and at the same time provided Absalom with information harmful to his cause.

But there must be a way to get the intelligence out of the palace to David's hideaway in the wilderness. Couriers were needed and David found them in the sons of the priests, Zadok and Abiathar. Zadok's son was Ahimaaz; Jonathan was Abiathar's son. Together these young men would stealthily shuttle information from Hushai to David.

The plan was now set. The operatives were in place. The stakes were high, but with God's help it just might work. If Hushai were discovered, it would certainly mean his death. And since David had involved the priesthood in espionage, the ramifications would be even greater if the priests' sons were caught. Everything must be kept secret. There could be no hitches.

It was pretty daring, trusting all of this to little people like Hushai, Ahimaaz and Jonathan. But David knew God frequently used little people to do big things. After all, the king had been a no-name shepherd boy when he slew the giant Goliath.

The Execution

The plan went off like clockwork. Here's how it happened.

Hushai returned to the palace, much to the surprise of Absalom. In fact, Absalom chided Hushai, "Is this your loyalty to your friend? Why did you not go with your friend?" (2 Sam. 16:17). Absalom thought it strange that such a close ally of his father did not flee with him. But Hushai played the role of the loyalist, saying, "No, but whom the LORD and this people and all the men of Israel choose, his will I be, and with him I will remain" (v. 18). The king was convinced. The secret agent was in!

Absalom wasted no time in seeking a strategy to harass and further humiliate his father. He must have hated David to want to hurt him so. Ahithophel was first to be asked for counsel. This turncoat had a two-phase plan of action.

Phase one was for Absalom to do something particularly disgusting that would show his superiority over his father and solidify the Israeli army behind him. Ahithophel's plan called for Absalom to sleep with his father's concubines. They had been left in the city to care for David's house. A tent was erected on top of the house so that this adultery would be committed in the sight of all Israel. Ahithophel knew Absalom would like this phase of his plan. Absalom could humiliate his father and establish himself as a ruthless ruler with this revolting act.

Phase two of Ahithophel's plan was to muster an elite corps of 12,000 men, led by Ahithophel, to pursue David and slay him, bringing all the others back to Jerusalem in peace. This would be a surgical attack, killing only God's anointed king. It would be neat, it would be quick, and it would be precise.

Actually, phase two of Ahithophel's plan wasn't bad strategy. It probably would have worked, but this is where Absalom made his fatal mistake. He called on Hushai to assess Ahithophel's plan, and, if it wasn't a good one, to advance one of his own. David's secret agent went right to work, boldly disputing the wisdom of Ahithophel's scheme on two fronts.

First, Hushai cautioned Absalom not to underestimate the ferocity of David's "mighty men." They loved their captain. They would fight to the death for David. Hushai described David and his men as a "bear robbed of her cub" (17:8). That bear would fight more ferociously than ever before and so would David's men.

Second, Hushai cautioned Absalom not to underestimate the cunning of David. After all, he was not some novice to warfare; he was the greatest military strategist of the day. David had proven his cunning before and he would most certainly do it again. David wouldn't be lodging with the troops but would surely be hiding in another place, perhaps a cave or a pit. Thus, if Absalom's forces surprised his entourage, David would surely be spared and would retaliate.

Absalom agreed. It made sense to him.

The king's secret agent had successfully thwarted the counsel of Ahithophel, but could he offer a battle plan that would sound equally fierce and just as certainly bring Absalom victory? No, he must do more. He must offer a plan so grandiose, so heinous that the proud Absalom would be sure to buy it. Hushai played on Absalom's hatred for his father and his thirst to destroy him.

Here was Hushai's counterplan.

Instead of selecting an elite force to engage in a surgical strike, Hushai counseled Absalom to gather all Israel together, from Dan to Beersheba, "like the sand that is by the sea for multitude" (v. 11). Hushai suggested Absalom muster the greatest army Israel had ever seen to engage in the largest battle Israel had ever seen.

Absalom liked that.

But Hushai's plan called for more. Whereas Ahithophel wanted to lead the elite corps of 12,000 men against David, Hushai told Absalom to lead the innumerable troops himself. Apparently Hushai wanted Absalom to reason, *Why should Ahithophel get the credit for defeating my father? I'll do it myself.*

Absalom liked that too.

Next, Hushai's plan called for the complete annihilation of David and his mighty men so that not a single soldier would survive the attack. This must be a complete victory over all of David's forces, not just a surgical victory over David himself. If David and his men were dead, they would never again threaten Absalom's authority.

Absalom liked that as well.

And finally, Hushai advised, if David is found hiding in a city, Absalom and his men should take ropes with them and completely destroy that city, drawing its stones into the river so that not one trace of the city that harbored David would remain. This must be an example to all who would defy Absalom's absolute rule.

Absalom really liked that.

It was settled. Absalom would follow the advice of Hushai. Perhaps we should ask ourselves why the ruthless Absalom opted for Hushai's battle strategy over Ahithophel's. The answer is obvious. Absalom wasn't thinking clearly because he was operating on the twin emotions of pride and hatred. He liked Hushai's plan better because it was more grandiose, more brutal, more despicable. The king's secret agent knew the wicked heart of Absalom would, given the chance, thirst for overkill. Hushai, David's counterspy in King Absalom's court, gave him that chance. Absalom wasn't just tricked into following Hushai's plan; this was the sovereignty of God at work.

Well, the rest of the story is history. Ahithophel returned to his home and hanged himself because Absalom had spurned his counsel. The delay caused by gathering all Israel to battle allowed David to escape. When Absalom finally pursued his father, Absalom's long, flowing hair got tangled in the branches of an oak tree and he was slain while swinging from the tree. David's loyalist troops were entirely victorious, and he returned to the palace in Jerusalem, where he rightfully belonged.

Once again right triumphed over wrong. But look who the hero of the story is: one of God's little people, Hushai, the secret agent to the king. He thwarted the purposes of evil because he remained loyal to God and to His king. While he resided in the court of Absalom, he was really in the palace of David.

In some ways we're like that too. We are on a mission—to thwart the purposes of Satan. We are in this world, but not of it (John 17:14). We live in the midst of the kingdom of darkness temporarily dominated by a usurper, but we serve the true King.

God can use you today just like He used Hushai. Guard your loyalties. Never trust the Absaloms of this world. Anticipate the King's return and work on His behalf until He does.

God's heroes aren't big people; they're little people whom God uses in a big way. Ask Hushai. He was one of God's champions, one of God's little people, people like you and me.

BARZILLAI

Name:	**Barzillai**
Nationality:	Gileadite
Era:	Circa 978 B.C.
Location:	Mahanaim in Gilead
Reference:	2 Samuel 17:27-29; 19:31-40; 1 Kings 2:7

Most Memorable Accomplishment:

Weary, hungry and desperate, David was on the run. His son Absalom had usurped the throne in Jerusalem and chased him across the Jordan River. Would David and his entourage starve in this foreign land? No. Enter Barzillai, a wealthy and aged man from Gilead who provided beds, basins and supplies for David's entire company—kind of a Middle Eastern Welcome Wagon. After Absalom was defeated, David wanted to repay this kindness and asked Barzillai to return to the palace with him. But the sensitive senior refused, opting to bestow those honors on his son instead. He is a fine example of Paul's exhortation, "Let each of you look out not only for his own interests, but also for the interests of others" (Phil. 2:4).

CHAPTER 6

Barzillai

The Generous Octogenarian

The teaching of Jesus Christ must have shocked the crowds that thronged around Him. Almost everything He taught them was diametrically opposed to what they believed and practiced. It's still true today.

For example, most of us think if only we were rich, all our problems would go away. But Jesus taught, "Woe to you who are rich" (Luke 6:24). It is innate to the human spirit to get those who get you. But Jesus said, "Love your enemies, do good to those who hate you" (v. 27). Should someone punch us in the mouth, we would likely punch back. But Jesus counseled, "To him who strikes you on the one cheek, offer the other also" (v. 29). Everything Jesus taught was so unfamiliar to those around Him.

In the context of these teachings the Lord posed some startling questions (vv. 32-34). Paraphrased, they are:

"If you love those who love you, what's the big deal?"

"If you do good to those who do good to you, so what?"

"If you lend to those whom you expect will repay you, what do you have to brag about?"

Everybody does these things!

Then, in light of this, the Lord asserted an inviolate rule: "Give, and it will be given to you: good measure, pressed down, shaken together, and running over will be put into your bosom. For with the same measure that you use, it will be measured back to you" (v. 38).

Giving is an act of kindness that should never be accompanied with the ulterior motive of getting in return. Our Heavenly Father demonstrated this. "For God so loved the world that He gave His only begotten Son, that whoever believes in Him should not perish but have everlasting life" (John 3:16). With love as His only motive, God gave His only Son to die for us so that we might have eternal life in heaven. God gained nothing in return. His giving was a pure act of kindness and love.

One of the little people of the Old Testament wonderfully demonstrates this principle. This is the story of Barzillai, the generous octogenarian.

During the dark period when Absalom usurped the throne from his father, David was on the run east of the Jordan River. He had a company of people with him, including his "mighty men" and many women and children as well. They would need food, shelter and clothing as they fled from Absalom. But this was the Transjordan; this was across the river. This was the territory of the Ammonites, with whom David had previously fought fierce battles. It wasn't likely he would find a friendly face and a hand outstretched in kindness here.

Enter Barzillai.

The story of Barzillai is recorded in three places in the Old Testament, documenting events that occurred on three separate occasions. For this reason, Barzillai's story is like a three-act play. It's a great story line. Let's enjoy the story of the generous octogenarian.

The lights dim and the curtain rises.

Act 1: A Deed of Kindness

There have been many famous trios throughout history: Shadrach, Meshech and Abednego; Caesar, Pompey and Crassus; Curley, Larry and Moe. But here is a trio that isn't famous at all—Shobi, Machir and Barzillai.

When David crossed the Jordan, he came to Mahanaim with Absalom right behind him. Suddenly, out of nowhere appeared Shobi, who lived in Rabbah in Ammon (which is

Amman, Jordan today); Machir, who lived in Lo Debar; and Barzillai, a Gileadite from Rogelim. This trio offered David and his followers beds to sleep on, plates and cups to eat and drink from, and a veritable smorgasbord of beans, lentils, grains, cheese, butter, mutton, honey and more. All this sounds like a modern Israeli breakfast.

These three strangers were not likely candidates to offer kindness to David. After all, when David committed his great sin with Bathsheba years earlier and sent her husband, Uriah, to the forefront of the battle so that he would be killed, that battle was the Jews of Jerusalem against the Ammonites of Rabbah (2 Sam. 11). Such battles were hard to forgive and even harder to forget.

Still, this unprecipitated act of kindness would not go unnoticed by the king-on-the-run. Barzillai and the others had exemplified the kind of spirit that would not be forgotten by the grateful David. They risked their necks, their fortunes and their futures by being kind to God's king. Then almost immediately they pass from the pages of Scripture.

Act 2: An Attempt to Repay Kindness

The conflict was over. Absalom had pursued his father to the death—his own death. Having caught his long, flowing hair in the branches of an oak tree, Absalom hung helplessly between heaven and earth. He made an easy target. Joab, the king's general, and his men slew David's son against David's wishes. The king's orders notwithstanding, Absalom was dead. It was now time for David to return home to his palace in Jerusalem and the throne given to him by God. His flight eastward was over; he was now making his way westward, back toward the Jordan and the Promised Land.

Again, enter Barzillai.

"And Barzillai the Gileadite came down from Rogelim and went across the Jordan with the king, to escort him across the Jordan" (2 Sam. 19:31). Here is another unprecipitated act of kindness.

Barzillai had everything to lose and nothing to gain when he had shown kindness to David earlier. Now, he may have had nothing to lose, but he certainly had nothing to gain by escorting the king back across the Jordan River on his way to Jerusalem and home. But kindness is a habit of life, not an isolated act. Barzillai had learned to deal kindly with all men, including Jews from Jerusalem.

With no request by Barzillai nor any prompting by anyone else, David decided to repay the kindness of his friend. The king said to Barzillai, "Come across with me, and I will provide for you while you are with me in Jerusalem" (v. 33). This was a royal invitation for Barzillai to enjoy the pleasures of the king's palace all the days of his life. It was the kind of invitation most people would snap up immediately. But not Barzillai.

Barzillai was a very wealthy man. Out of his abundance he had fed David and his troops earlier. But historically, he was a nobody who had come out of nowhere to show the deposed king a little kindness. Barzillai could have accepted the king's generous offer. He had sustained David when the king was in great need. Why not allow David to sustain him now?

But Barzillai had not acted in kindness toward David to receive a reward. He had acted out of compassion and concern. Therefore, he refused the king's offer on the grounds that he was old and he wouldn't live long. Besides, this 80-year-old had lost much of his ability to taste the delicacies that would be served at David's table. Neither could he hear the singing of the young men and women who would entertain at mealtime. Age was catching up with him. Why should he become a burden to David? He hadn't shown kindness to the king to become a millstone around David's neck.

Even though Barzillai would return to his own city to die, this generous octogenarian would show his generosity and kindness one more time—this time to his son. To David he said, "But here is your servant Chimham; let him cross over with my lord the king, and do for him what shall seem good to you" (v. 37)

The matter was settled. David was permitted to repay the act of kindness Barzillai had shown to him, and this sensitive senior citizen was able to give another kindness in the process.

Barzillai is a perfect example of what Paul had in mind when he said, "Let each of you look out not only for his own interests, but also for the interests of others" (Phil. 2:4). We are to be as interested in the welfare of others as we are in our own welfare.

So the king kissed Barzillai and blessed him. The old man returned to his city to die in peace. David returned to his city to one day do the same.

Again Barzillai passes from the pages of Scripture.

Act 3: A Command to Repay Kindness

Toward the end of David's life he began to make serious preparations for the continuance of his kingdom. He called Solomon to his side in order to instruct the man who would be king in the ways of governance and the ways of God.

Then David assembled all the princes of Israel together in Jerusalem. He stood and recalled how he had planned to build a permanent dwelling place for God, but because he was a man of war God reserved that privilege for his son Solomon. David praised the Lord before the whole congregation and said, "Blessed are you, LORD God of Israel, our Father, for ever and ever. Yours, O LORD, is the greatness, the power, and the glory, the victory and the majesty" (1 Chron. 29:10-11). It was a very public and joyous occasion.

But David also gave Solomon some private instructions about the treatment of individuals after he died (1 Kings 2). Some of these instructions admittedly are difficult for us to understand. But that's because we live in an era that has historically had the morality of Christ as its cornerstone. In David's day it was strictly "an eye for an eye."

Tucked away in David's instructions to Solomon is a frequently missed reference to one of God's little people—Barzillai. David said, "But show kindness to the sons of Barzillai the Gileadite, and let them be among those who eat at your table, for so they came to me when I fled from Absalom your brother" (1 Kings 2:7).

Determined to repay the kindness that Barzillai had shown to him years earlier, the dying king wanted to be sure that Barzillai's heirs were well cared for. Preparing to die means much more than making funeral arrangements. There are spiritual preparations—making sure you are on your way to heaven. There are financial preparations—making sure your family and God's work are remembered in your estate. And there are personal preparations—making sure those who have been kind to you are adequately thanked in your death even as they were in your life. David was the king, a big person. He made all these preparations. So should little people like you and me.

The Legacy

When faced with the opportunity to show kindness, never hesitate to do so. To give to others with the right motives is to give to God. And one thing is for sure: you can't outgive God. As Scripture reminds us, "Honor the Lord with your possessions, and with the firstfruits of all your increase; so your barns will be filled with plenty, and your vats will overflow with new wine" (Prov. 3:9-10).

Kindness is never out of fashion. Repay kindness with kindness. It's the legacy of kings like David and commoners like Barzillai. It also should be the legacy of people like you and me. Leave behind you a legacy that will be a model for another generation. Kindness costs, but it also pays.

ITTAI

Name:	**Ittai**
Nationality:	Gittite
Era:	Circa 979 B.C.
Location:	Judean Wilderness, east of Jerusalem
Reference:	2 Samuel 15:18-22; 18:2, 5

Most Memorable Accomplishment:

Sometimes when false friends abandon you, true friends are discovered. And often they are discovered under some of the most unusual circumstances. When David was driven from his palace in Jerusalem by his son Absalom, he was accompanied by an unlikely ally, Ittai the Gittite. Although he hailed from the city of David's vanquished foe, Goliath, Ittai showed unswerving loyalty to the king. Even when David suggested several legitimate excuses that Ittai could have used for staying behind in Jerusalem, he still chose to be with the man of God in the wilderness rather than the man of power in the palace. When David's fortunes turned, he rewarded Ittai's loyalty by naming him captain over one-third of his armies.

CHAPTER 7

Ittai

The Man Who Wouldn't Return

"Oh, that I were made judge in the land, and everyone who has any suit or cause would come to me; then I would give him justice" (2 Sam. 15:4). How could anyone fall for that line? It was nothing but the sickening-sweet syrup of a spiritual sissy. But it worked. With those sentiments, Absalom stole the hearts of Israel away from his father, the man after God's own heart.

Absalom was not content as the king's son; he wanted to be king. He was quick to point out the deficiencies in David's government. No one was appointed as a judge to hear matters that were disputed between common citizens. Absalom was equally quick to suggest that he was the perfect candidate for the job. As his popularity increased, he gathered counselors around him and conspired to dethrone David and drive him out of Jerusalem.

When a messenger brought the news to David, the king had but one choice. He must hastily flee from his palace and the capital. As in the days of Saul, David was on the run again.

Preparations for travel were brief. They took only what they could carry. David evacuated his family, closest aids and servants. Others loyal to him were allowed to come along, but they were not encouraged.

Almost immediately David was gone. His entourage met at a prearranged place in the wilderness where they would be safe until they could regroup. It was at this wilderness rendezvous that we are introduced to the man who wouldn't return. His name was Ittai the Gittite.

Ittai is one of those unlikely heroes, someone who bursts onto the pages of history unannounced, but leaves a mark that cannot go unnoticed. He's one of God's little people—people just like you and me.

Here's his story.

Ittai's Unlikely Alliance

There have been many strange alliances in history. Some of them are recorded in the Bible. For example, the alliance between Joseph and the great pharaoh of Egypt was unlikely. Who would have thought that a Jewish slave boy would rise to become the prime minister of Egypt? Joseph wasn't the Wall Street type.

And what about the alliance between Peter and John? John was gentle, quiet and retiring. Peter was flamboyant, boisterous and aggressive. Still, the two apostles frequently appear together in Scripture: preparing the upper room, running to the empty tomb, going to the temple to pray. They were complete opposites and unlikely allies, but they were inseparable.

Politics also makes some pretty unlikely alliances. This is the basis of the expression "Politics makes strange bedfellows." Ronald Reagan and George Bush were often on opposite sides of the political fence. Bush coined the description of Reagan's famous "trickle-down economics" as "voodoo economics." Still, in 1980 they became running mates, then served eight years together as president and vice president of the United States, respectively.

Ittai's alliance with David was perhaps the most unlikely of all. As the deposed king fled to his hiding place in the wilderness, he noticed that Ittai the Gittite and his family were accompanying him. "And the king said to Ittai the Gittite, 'Why are you also going with us? Return and remain'" (2 Sam. 15:19).

What makes the alliance between Ittai the Gittite and David the Israelite so unlikely? Everyone knows of David's great victory over the giant Goliath. It was common knowledge, even in his day. It is the stuff of which legends are made. Goliath was the champion of the city of Gath, and David had defeated him.

A resident of California is a Californian. A resident of Texas is a Texan. A resident of Maine is a Mainer (not a Maniac). But do you know what you call a resident of Gath?

A few chapters later in 2 Samuel, a battle is recorded between the Philistines and the Israelites at a place called Gob. Specific mention is made of a Bethlehemite named Elhanan who slew a giant, the brother of Goliath the Gittite (21:19).

What do you call a resident of Gath? You call him a Gittite!

Ittai lived in the city of Gath and only recently had come to Jerusalem. He hailed from the village whose champion had been humiliated and killed in battle by David. Why would he align himself with David? Why would he be loyal to the great enemy of his hometown, especially now that the once-powerful king was on the run? This is an unlikely alliance indeed.

Ittai's Unused Alibi

Ittai's alliance with the Hebrew king even puzzled David. He questioned, "Why are you also going with us?" (15:19). It just didn't make any sense. Why would a Gittite tag along with an Israelite? His intentions appeared honorable enough, but were they wise?

Ittai had thrown in his lot with David instead of Absalom. While it proved to be the right decision, at the time it was not a very logical decision. Had he chosen to side with Absalom in this intra-Israelite dispute, he could have remained in Jerusalem in safety. Instead, he fled to the wilderness with the apparent loser in this power struggle.

Did Ittai have to accompany David? Of course not. He had several good alibis for not taking this course of action. What were they? David summarized them.

"For you are a foreigner and also an exile" (v. 19). David seems to be saying, "Ittai, you don't have to come with me. You're not even an Israelite. You're a foreigner. No one would expect you to take sides in a dispute like this, especially not my side!" But Ittai did.

Again David said, "In fact, you came only yesterday" (v. 20). Not only was Ittai not Jewish and not a permanent resident of Jerusalem, but he had come to the city only the day before. He was new in town. What an unfortunate circumstance—to arrive in a foreign capital on the very day there was a coup d'etat!

Ittai could have waited out the political instability in Jerusalem. After all, he had two good alibis. He was not an Israelite, and he arrived in Jerusalem only yesterday. But he had another good excuse. Second Samuel 15:22 mentions "all the little ones who were with him."

David reasoned with Ittai, "If you won't think of yourself, Ittai, at least think of the women and children with you. Why deny them the comforts of home and endanger their lives?" Ittai was a warrior, but he had his family and others in his entourage. If his loyalty to David would allow him to endanger his own life, that's one thing. But could that loyalty be so strong as to endanger his family? Shouldn't his family considerations be his strongest?

This same reasoning is often used on those who commit their lives to serve God on the mission field. "Why do you deprive your family and yourself of the good life? You have many reasons to stay at home. Give your kids a 'normal' life." There are always reasons for not obeying the will of God in your life, but there are never good ones.

Ittai had all the alibis he needed, but he didn't use any of them. Why? Because he had determined to go where God was blessing. And while Israel's people were with Absalom, it was evident that Israel's God was with David. There is great wisdom in hanging out where God is blessing.

Ittai's Unswerving Allegiance

Although David saw little reason for Ittai to risk his life in fleeing with him, Ittai displayed a rock-solid allegiance to the deposed king. His pledge was, "As the LORD lives, and as my lord the king lives, surely in whatever place my lord the king shall be, whether in death or in life, even there also your servant will be" (v. 21).

Doesn't this remind you of another unlikely alliance? Naomi and Ruth had both experienced the pain of loss. They were mother-in-law and daughter-in-law, both widows. When Naomi suggested Ruth remain in her native Moab and not accompany her back to Israel, Ruth said, "Entreat me not to leave you, or to turn back from following after you; for wherever you go, I will go; and wherever you lodge, I will lodge; your people shall be my people, and your God, my God" (Ruth 1:16). In this respect, Ittai is the male counterpart of Ruth in the Bible.

What causes such allegiance? What had this Gittite seen in David that the Israelites failed to see? Did Ittai see the possibility of future reward for aligning himself with David? Not likely. It appeared that David would never return to power and would be disgraced forever. Ittai evidently had nothing to gain from his allegiance.

But that's what many say today about Christians. There is nothing to gain by a loyal allegiance to Jesus Christ. The gold is in the palace, not in the tent of the wanderer. The prestige is in Jerusalem, not in the wilderness of Judea. The way to get ahead, say some, is to play the game with the back-stabber types like Absalom, not with the guileless types like David.

But Ittai was one of God's heroes, one who had learned that blessing comes from God. If his life was to be blessed, Ittai knew his allegiance had to be focused on those who demonstrated allegiance to God. He decided to do what he knew was right, even if no one else followed him. He would not forsake the rightful king, for David had not forsaken God.

Though the king's resources were scarce and his group was small, Ittai knew that David had one thing going for him that Absalom did not. David had remained true to Jehovah, and Ittai must as well. His unswerving allegiance did not grow out of love for comfort or gain, but out of love for David and his God.

Is there a lesson here for the Christian today? Absolutely. Doing what is right should not be deterred by circumstances. Ittai was a Gittite. Ittai had solid alibis for not accompanying David. Still, his allegiance was strong because David represented what was right, while Absalom represented what was wrong.

For the Christian the question is never, Shall I do right or wrong? The question is, Do I have the courage to do what is right even if everyone else does what is wrong? Ittai answered that question with a resounding yes!

Ittai's Ultimate Advancement

Do you think God has a short memory? Do you think He forgot about the treachery of Absalom? More to the point, do you think He forgot about the courage of Ittai?

God keeps good records. His rewards are commensurate with our faithfulness in service. He is perfectly just and eager to advance us; He is looking for loyalty and obedience.

It wasn't long until Absalom's ill-fated coup had ended. He chased his father from Jerusalem and throughout Judea, the Jordan Valley and the Transjordan. But God protected His man and David escaped the treachery of his son. The same was not true for Absalom. Eventually he was disgraced and shamefully killed.

Note, however, that while God was demoting Absalom, who chose the popular path of wrong, He was promoting Ittai, who chose the more demanding path of right. Second Samuel 18 begins by recording, "And David numbered the people who were with him, and set captains of thousands and captains of hundreds over them" (v. 1).

Even though he was on the run, David would have to defend himself against the attacks of his usurper son. He therefore organized his army of people into a people's army in exile. This army would need leadership, a few good men who were loyal to David and his God. It would need generals who showed unshakable allegiance. It would need the best people David had, loyal and obedient.

"Then David sent out one third of the people under the hand of Joab, one third under the hand of Abishai the son of Zeruiah, Joab's brother, and one-third under the hand of Ittai the Gittite" (v. 2).

Imagine it. A Gittite, a resident of the same city as the giant Goliath, would command one-third of David's army. Wouldn't that be risky for the deposed king? Not at all. Ittai had proven himself in a simple act of allegiance when allegiance was not popular. David knew Ittai would be trustworthy in more responsibility as well.

It Pays to Do Right

Ittai's ultimate advancement came as a direct result of doing what was right, even when everyone else was doing what was wrong. The hearts of all Israel were drawn away from God's man because of the honey-dipped words of a smooth-talking charlatan.

But that happens every day, doesn't it? People just like you and me are daily exposed to Satan's clever promises and schemes. If we would just align ourselves with God, however, if we would just show unswerving allegiance to Him, if we would just follow those who follow Him, how much better off we would be. Those who forsook David and followed Absalom not only missed out on Absalom's promises, but they also missed out on David's promotions.

Does it pay to do what is right? Absolutely. Does it pay even if everyone else is doing what is wrong? Ittai knew the answer. It is usually easy to do what is right when all our friends do the same. It is easy when we are in church, with others doing what pleases God. But Ittai is one of those heroes who teaches us that it pays to do right even if no one else joins us.

Every one who wishes to please God awaits the day when we will hear Christ say, "Well done, good and faithful servant; you were faithful over a few things, I will make you ruler over many things. Enter into the joy of your lord" (Matt. 25:21). Ittai must have rejoiced when he heard similar words from David.

Ittai the Gittite was an insignificant exile who arrived in town on the worst possible day. But he quickly sized up the situation and knew that to be blessed of God he had to go where

God was blessing. He followed David into the wilderness, showed an unshakable allegiance to him and was rewarded because of it. He was a nobody whom God made a somebody.

Will God do any less for you?

EBED-MELECH

Name:	**Ebed-Melech**
Nationality:	Ethiopian
Era:	Circa 588 B.C.
Location:	Jerusalem
Reference:	Jeremiah 38:1-13; 39:15-18

Most Memorable Accomplishment:

Jeremiah had predicted the downfall of Jerusalem just as God had revealed to him. For this he was cast into a muddy cistern in the court of the guardhouse. He would have died there, sinking in the mire, had it not been for one Ethiopian hero. Ebed-Melech, a court eunuch, went to the king and protested the injustice done to the prophet. Such an act could have meant Ebed-Melech's life. Instead, the king entrusted to him the responsibility to save Jeremiah's life. Resourcefully, Ebed-Melech used old, worn-out clothes and rags to protect Jeremiah's arms from rope burns as they pulled him out of the pit. Why? Because it was all he had. Heroes must be resourceful as well as courageous.

CHAPTER 8

Ebed-Melech

An All-Ethiopian Hero

In the winter of 1982, an Air Florida jet took off from the Washington National Airport, now the Ronald Reagan National Airport. It was a very cold day—so cold, in fact, that planes were having difficulty keeping ice from forming on their wings. The Air Florida jet had been de-iced, but unknown to anyone the ice had reformed. Within seconds of take-off it was evident the plane was having difficulty gaining altitude. It flew so low that it hit a crowded bridge and plummeted into the Potomac River.

Those who remember that cold day also recall seeing live coverage of the tragedy unfolding. Washington, D.C., news crews were on the scene almost immediately. Many lives were lost, but many also were saved. A crowd gathered on the banks of the Potomac to watch. They stood in shock and horror at what they saw. Dead bodies and live victims floated together in the icy waters. Suddenly, as if overwhelmed by the terror unfolding before him, an unknown man in the crowd jumped into the water, swam to victim after victim and safely returned to the bank with them. He nearly died from exhaustion, but he had little regard for his own safety. Something had to be done, and he knew he must do it. Only later did we come to learn his name. Lenny Skutnik instantly became an all-American hero.

What makes someone do such a thing? Why would a man jump into swift waters filled with chunks of ice, pieces of debris from the airplane and dead bodies to rescue those who survived? These were people he had never met before, total strangers to him. What kind of a man does an act of courage like that take? Whatever the answer, there are many little people like

Lenny Skutnik who courageously respond during a life-threatening tragedy. Some of them are mentioned in the Bible.

The Forgotten Ethiopian Eunuch

Do you know the story of the Ethiopian eunuch? If I asked you to put this book aside, pick up your Bible and turn to the story of the Ethiopian eunuch, would you know where it is located in the Bible? Even if you don't know off the top of your head, can you recall the story? Who were the main characters? What was the story all about?

Well, if you answered that the story of the Ethiopian eunuch is found in Acts 8, you'd be right. And if you said this is the story of a man traveling from Jerusalem to Gaza who was reading Isaiah 53 but didn't understand what he was reading, again you'd be right. And if you knew the main characters were the eunuch and Philip the evangelist, I'd be impressed with your Bible knowledge. But while you would be absolutely right, you would also be entirely wrong.

While the eunuch from Ethiopia whose story is recorded in Acts 8 is not a major figure in Bible history, at least he is recognizable and you know his story. But what if I told you there is another eunuch mentioned in the Bible? What if you knew he was an Ethiopian? If you were asked to tell the story of the Old Testament Ethiopian eunuch, could you do it? "An Old Testament Ethiopian eunuch?" you question. "Didn't know there was such a character." Most people don't.

This Ethiopian eunuch is the Lenny Skutnik of the Bible, a little-known person whose story you would never know had he been able to stand by and watch the prophet Jeremiah waste away in a horrible pit. This Old Testament Ethiopian eunuch is truly one of God's heroes, one of the little people of the Bible who served a big God. Let's get to know him better, and maybe we'll see something of ourselves in him. His story is found in Jeremiah 38.

The Ethiopian's Story

Jeremiah was not a very popular prophet, as often faithful

prophets aren't. The last days of Jewish freedom were coming to an end. God was about to judge Judah for forgetting Him and living in immorality and disobedience. Jeremiah is frequently called the "weeping prophet" because he wept over the sins of his people. We could use more like him today. He was raised up by God to warn the government and the people that Jehovah would not tolerate continued rebellion against Him. Often Jeremiah's message was seen as negative and therefore unwanted and unheeded.

Things are no different today. People like positive messages from our pulpits, but God often requires His faithful prophets to give just the opposite, to lash out at sin and warn of judgment. That was Jeremiah's lot. He had to warn Judah that God would use the hated Babylonians to bring judgment on His covenant people. There was no way to stop God's judgment, and thus there was no way to stop Nebuchadnezzar and the mighty Babylonians.

Because Jeremiah's message was perceived as unpatriotic, unflattering and unthinkable, he was apprehended by the king's guard and cast into a dungeon owned by the king's son. There the prophet was left to die. And he would have died, had it not been for the courage of an all-Ethiopian hero named Ebed-Melech.

When the eunuch heard about Jeremiah's imprisonment, be became concerned for the prophet's safety in the muddy pit. Bravely he went to the king's house and pleaded with the king to spare Jeremiah's life. It worked. Zedekiah, the king, commanded Ebed-Melech to hustle off and save Jeremiah from the dungeon. The eunuch took some old rags to put under Jeremiah's arms, tied them together, lowered them with a rope into the pit and pulled the prophet to safety. Like the man who jumped into the icy waters of the Potomac, Ebed-Melech had to think fast and act fast if Jeremiah was to live another day.

In a nutshell, that's the story of this little-known hero. But what of the man himself? What kind of man would be this brave? What kind of man would stick his neck out for an unpopular prophet? What qualities are unmistakable in Ebed-Melech's character, qualities that you and I should look deeply within our own lives to find today? Let's take a closer look at what kind of man this all-Ethiopian hero was.

A Concerned Man

We live in a very "care less" society today. Regardless of what happens, most people couldn't care less. When the president of the United States was accused of having an affair with a White House intern, his popularity soared in the polls. People couldn't care less about immoral living and suspected infidelity. When a Korean shopkeeper in Los Angeles was robbed and beaten within an inch of his life, no one was willing to dial 911. When a young Detroit girl was involved in a minor fender bender, pursued by the other driver, stopped on a bridge and beaten, she chose to jump to her death in the waters below rather than be murdered. Dozens of motorists sat in their cars and watched it all happen. They couldn't have cared less.

This "care less" attitude was first burned in the American consciousness decades ago when a young woman named Kitty Genovese was brutally stabbed on a New York City street. As horrific as the crime was, it was made even worse because Miss Genovese cried out repeatedly, "I'm dying! I'm dying!" during the 35-minute attack, and yet the windows facing the street were closed and lights went out as not one of her neighbors lifted a finger to help her. More than 30 respectable people heard the blood-curdling screams, but Kitty Genovese died because no one wanted to get involved. Had Lenny Skutnik not wanted to get involved, many more would have died when that Air Florida jet crashed into the Potomac. And had Ebed-Melech not wanted to get involved, Jeremiah the prophet would have suffocated in the mud of a Jerusalem pit.

A lack of concern for the injustices done to those around us has been a hallmark of sinful man right from the beginning. Joseph's brothers had no regard for his welfare when they threw him into a pit and later sold him into slavery (Gen. 37:20-28). One of the saddest stories recorded in the Bible is one of homosexual lust and heterosexual callousness when a woman was abused all night and her husband had no regard for her sanctity, her safety or her life (Judg. 19:1-26). And isn't a lack of concern for the welfare of others the basis for the story of the Good Samaritan (Luke 10:30-37)?

But it was just the opposite for Ebed-Melech, the Ethiopian eunuch. His concern for the prophet sparked his efforts to save Jeremiah's life. Ebed-Melech couldn't stand by and do nothing when Jeremiah was sinking in the mud of that pit. He demonstrated that his concern was more than skin-deep when he went to the king to plead for Jeremiah's life.

I wonder how concerned you and I are when we see someone who needs our help. When there's a family in the church who hasn't eaten adequately the previous week, do you invite them to join you for Sunday dinner? Do you share some of your groceries with them? When a neighbor loses his job and you know of a job at your company that requires his skills, do you inquire about it for him, or do you nonchalantly say, "Let him check the help wanted section of the papers"? When a widow in the church needs some repairs on her roof before winter and you learn about it, do you wish her luck, or are you concerned enough to inquire how you might help?

In a seaside area where ships often crashed on the rocks in violent weather was a harbor town widely known for its dedicated rescue team. Whenever the siren sounded, men and women rushed to the scene and risked life and limb to save the drowning sailors. After several years the people had enough money to build a rescue station close to the shore. Some of them even took special training in first aid and CPR. As time went by, they added some comforts and conveniences to the station, furnishing it with a lounge and a kitchen, then a bar and sleeping quarters. Finally it became a club where the townspeople gathered to have fun and mingle with each other. The alarm still sounded, but nobody responded. They were reluctant to leave their comforts and pleasures just to save lives. People were drowning offshore, but nobody was concerned.

Sometimes our comfort and safety contribute to our lack of concern for others, and a lack of concern usually leads to the deadly disease known as "hardening of the attitudes." Ebed-Melech was a hero in God's eyes because he was a concerned man. Godly character always produces genuine concern.

A Courageous Man

Concern for those in need is a good place to start, but it's never enough by itself. It's commendable to be concerned, but Good Samaritans do more than express concern; they take action. Ebed-Melech was concerned enough about Jeremiah's life that he put his own life on the line for the prophet.

Don't lose sight of the fact that this man was a eunuch and an Ethiopian living in the court of the Jewish king, Zedekiah. A eunuch was a male servant of the royal household, emasculated by castration as a precautionary measure, especially if he served among the wives in the ruler's harem (2 Kings 9:32). Being an Ethiopian, he was likely a slave to the Jewish king. It was not like Ebed-Melech was a golfing buddy of Zedekiah. He was a nobody who existed to serve the needs of the palace. Still, his concern for Jeremiah wouldn't let him rest. He had to do something. Have you ever felt that way about something that is really important?

Jeremiah 38:8-9 records, "Ebed-Melech went out of the king's house and spoke to the king, saying: 'My lord the king, these men have done evil in all that they have done to Jeremiah the prophet, whom they have cast into the dungeon, and he is likely to die from hunger in the place where he is. For there is no more bread in the city.'"

The eunuch approached his king at the Gate of Benjamin and poured out his heart to him. He was polite, kind, respectful and direct. He didn't beat around the bush. He didn't equivocate. Ebed-Melech must have been trembling as he made a moral judgment on what the people had done to Jeremiah. Today he would be considered part of a "right-wing conservative conspiracy" in society. To God, he was just a concerned man showing incredible courage.

Ebed-Melech wasn't the first, of course, to show this kind of courage in standing before a king or magistrate to speak out for what was right. Moses stood before Pharaoh and said, "Let my people go" (Ex. 5:1). Nathan stood before King David and said, "You are the man!" (2 Sam. 12:7). Nor would Ebed-Melech be the last to show this kind of courage. Esther stood before King Ahasuerus and said, "My people and I [are] . . . to be killed" (Esther 7:4). Daniel stood before King Belshazzar and said, "You have been weighed in the balances, and found wanting" (Dan. 5:27). Peter stood before the high priest and said, "We ought to obey God rather than men" (Acts 5:29).

Sometimes, however, it takes more courage to stand up for the Lord before a university professor who belittles anyone who believes the creation account of Scripture than it takes to stand before a king. Sometimes it takes more courage to confront a friend who is living in adultery than it does to stand before a high priest. You may never stand before a grand jury or a judge or a president or premier for your faith, but almost daily you have need to be as courageous as Ebed-Melech in your relationship with others.

Standing up for the unborn can jeopardize your job, but concern for human life must be translated into courage. Taking a stand against pornography on cable TV or at the local newsstand requires courage. Your situation may be different from Ebed-Melech's, but the need for courageous action isn't. Little people can make a big difference when they take their courage from a big God.

A Trusted Man

As remarkable as this eunuch's courage was, equally remarkable was the king's response to Ebed-Melech's concern. Jeremiah 38:10 says, "Then the king commanded Ebed-Melech the Ethiopian, saying, 'Take from here thirty men with you, and lift Jeremiah the prophet out of the dungeon before he dies.'" That was a pretty dramatic turnaround for this man. There is recorded no royal dissent or anxiety when Jeremiah was placed in the palace dungeon, but now hurriedly Zedekiah commanded that the prophet be rescued before he died.

Have you ever considered that the very issue you're concerned about in your church or your community may be corrected immediately if you had the courage to express your concern? If the curriculum in your child's school teaches that homosexual and lesbian lifestyles are normal and that concerns you, have you had the courage to speak to the school board president? Maybe the situation would change as easily as Jeremiah's did when Ebed-Melech showed enough courage to approach the king. If you're concerned about the way your church is spending more money on programs than on getting the Gospel to people, get up enough courage to talk to someone in leadership about it. Maybe your polite, kind, respectful, direct expression of concern is all that is necessary to set the wheels of change in motion. The key is to link courage to your concern.

But when you express your concern and the pastor or school board president asks you to sit on a task force or to help him to look into the problem, don't melt away like snow on the Fourth of July. Courageous people usually are trusted people. Our little-known hero, Ebed-Melech, was immediately sized up by the king as a man he could trust to do what was right. If Jeremiah was to be saved, Ebed-Melech would be the man to do it. The king gave him that responsibility because he instantly trusted him.

Again, there are plenty of biblical precedents that show that courageous people are often entrusted with action because of their courage. Take Abraham's servant, for example. Abraham had 318 trained servants in his household (Gen. 14:14), but none of them was more trusted than Eliezer of Damascus. When the patriarch wanted to find a wife for his son, Isaac, he sent his trusted servant to Mesopotamia to find the right woman (Gen. 24). When David needed a friend with whom to trust his life, he chose the courageous and faithful Jonathan, even though he was the son of David's worst enemy (1 Sam. 20). Paul entrusted the care of the churches to young Timothy (1 Thess. 3:1-2) with the exhortation that "God has not given us a spirit of fear, but of power and of love and of a sound mind" (2 Tim. 1:7).

Courageous people tend to be trusted people. When the pastor needs someone to respond quickly to a difficult situation in the church, are you the one he calls on? When the dean needs a student to represent the college or seminary, are you the one he thinks of first? When an older woman in the church needs someone to visit her, perhaps to read the Word to her, are you the one the church entrusts with that opportunity? When a young mother needs a baby-sitter so she can get away for a couple of hours and attend a Bible study, are you trustworthy enough for the job? When God needs a courageous servant to carry the Gospel to the ends of the earth, will He think of you? Are you trusted with the big tasks because you have proven yourself courageous and trustworthy with the little tasks?

King Zedekiah entrusted Ebed-Melech with the task of saving Jeremiah's life because who better to trust than the only one who was concerned about the prophet's life and courageous enough to say something about it? Amazing, isn't it, how there is such an evident link between concern, courage and trust? If you want to be entrusted with responsibility, show the courage needed to express your concerns.

But there's one more observation about this Ethiopian eunuch that jumps out of his story at us. He's not one of those big-name people in the Bible, but he was a hero. Here's part of the reason why.

With a rescue team of 30 men, Ebed-Melech rushed to the dungeon in the king's house under the treasury and found Jeremiah sinking in the mud and mire. If the prophet was to be saved, they'd have to hurry. What could Ebed-Melech use to rescue Jeremiah?

The Ethiopian eunuch looked around and found some cast-off clothes and old rags. The King James Version calls them "old cast clouts and rotten rags." They were all Ebed-Melech had, and the resourceful eunuch used these worthless, worn-out rags to save the prophet's life. He told his 30 helpers to send the old rags down into the cistern with a rope to pull Jeremiah out of the mud. Then he said to the prophet, "Please put these old clothes and rags under your armpits, under the ropes" (v. 12), and with these seemingly worthless cast-off remnants, they pulled Jeremiah to safety.

It's hard to decide what in this story is the most astounding. Was it the concern Ebed-Melech had for a dying man? Was it his courage that enabled him to stand before the most powerful man in Judah and express his concern? Was it the fact that the king immediately entrusted the prophet's rescue to a lowly slave? Or was it the extraordinary resourcefulness of Ebed-Melech to use what he had on hand to save the prophet's life?

Perhaps the most useful lesson we can glean from the story of this little-known Bible hero is that we must use whatever God places at our disposal for His glory. When Moses balked at the idea of being God's spokesman to stand before Pharaoh, the "I AM" God asked him, "What is that in your hand?" (Ex. 4:2). Whatever we have in our hands, whatever we have at our disposal, whatever it is God has given to us, whether large or small, He expects us to use to accomplish the task He has given us.

For Samson it was the jawbone of a donkey. It wasn't much; certainly it wasn't a carefully crafted weapon, but it was enough with God's help to kill 1,000 Philistines (Judg. 15:15). For David it was a sling. Again, not a product of military intelligence, but it was all David had in his hand. With that crude little sling David killed the gigantic Goliath, who came to him with a sword, a spear and a javelin (1 Sam. 17:40-51). For a little lad in the crowd listening to Jesus one day, it was five barley loaves and two small fish. It's all he had; it's what God had placed at his disposal. But with that tiny lunch, willingly given to the Master, 5,000 hungry people were fed (John 6:9-12). And for a widow it was just two brass coins, the widow's mites, almost worthless. But out of concern for the needs of others, she courageously gave all she had, and God rewarded her resourcefulness by recording her story in Mark 12 with unusual praise.

A great deal of our service to the Lord arises out of simple resourcefulness. What has God given you? What is in your hand? What is lying around the house, or what skills has He given you that can be used for Him? Take note, because whatever God put into you He expects to get out; that's why He gave it to you.

Look around you. Do you think there isn't much you can do for God? Ebed-Melech probably thought that way too. After all, he was an emasculated Ethiopian slave serving humbly in a foreign king's court. He had little or nothing going for him but concern and courage, which produced trust and the opportunity to be resourceful in doing a big work for God.

Take stock in yourself and your assets. What do you have? Can you sing? The church choir likely needs you. Can you play the piano, even a little? There's a retirement home nearby who would love to have you volunteer to play hymns for the residents. Can you use a word processor? Mission agencies, churches and ministries always need volunteers with computer skills. Can you drive? Likely there is a shut-in at church who could use you a couple of days a week either to take her to the store or to pick up things for her. Can you do that? Be resourceful. Your greatest ministry may be hiding just beneath a small ability.

It doesn't take long to compile a list of the things each of us could do if we were sufficiently concerned about others. What will be on your list? What do you have with which you can show God your resourcefulness? Remember, God expects us to use what we have. He won't give us more until we do.

I can't help but believe that if Ebed-Melech had been on the bank of the Potomac River that frigid day in 1982, there would have been two men jumping into the water to save the lives of those who were perishing. Ebed-Melech was just like most heroes. They don't leave their house in the morning saying, "Today I think I'll be a hero." They are just ordinary people who have a concern for others, the courage to do something about that concern, the character to be trusted with important tasks and the resourcefulness to use whatever they have at hand to be successful.

Ebed-Melech is one of God's little people. He's the Ethiopian eunuch whom nobody remembers. In fact, take your Bible dictionary, look up "Ethiopian eunuch" or just "eunuch," and see if it tells the story of the Acts 8 Ethiopian eunuch but fails to mention one of God's great heroes, the Jeremiah 38 Ethiopian eunuch. That's okay. Like many of God's champions, the world may forget your name, but God never does. Ebed-Melech was one of God's little people—people just like you and me. What God did through him, He can do through you too. Be ready!

ONESIPHORUS

Name:	**Onesiphorus**
Nationality:	Greek
Era:	A.D. 67
Location:	Ephesus / Rome
Reference:	2 Timothy 1:16-18; 4:19

Most Memorable Accomplishment:

Someone once said that a true friend is a person who walks in when the rest of the world walks out. Onesiphorus was that kind of a friend. When we first encounter his name in 2 Timothy, Paul's life was drawing to a close. He had been arrested in Jerusalem, held prisoner in Caesarea for a couple of years and finally shipped off to Rome. After remaining under house arrest in Rome for another two years, he was finally released. But his freedom was short-lived. After a brief journey to Macedonia and most likely to Spain, Paul was arrested again and imprisoned at Rome. During this time "all those in Asia" turned away from him (2 Tim. 1:15)—all, that is, except for Onesiphorus. Just as he had befriended Paul in Ephesus, Onesiphorus stood by his friend in Rome. When all the world walked out, Onesiphorus walked in. When Paul thought of Onesiphorus, he thought of a friend who "often refreshed me" (v. 16). All of us would love a friend like that.

CHAPTER 9

Onesiphorus

The Friend
Who Refreshes

When you think of a friend, whom do you think of? What face comes to mind? Is it a friendly face? A refreshing face? A loving face? How would you define a friend? Someone has said that a friend is one who knows all about you and likes you just the same. Do you know somebody like that? A friend is someone who does his knocking before he enters instead of after he leaves. We could all use someone like that.

A friend is a person with whom you may think aloud. You have no secrets from a true friend. A friend is somebody who makes you do your best. Friends help us raise our life a notch or two. They refresh us when we are depleted, discouraged and distressed.

Onesiphorus was all of that and much more. He was a friend whom Paul found "refreshing." Friendship is a gentle breeze on a sultry day. It's cool water to a thirsty man. Onesiphorus knew how to lift the spirits and encourage the heart of his friend. Among the many acquaintances Paul made on his missionary journeys, his friendship with Onesiphorus stood out.

But who is this friend of the apostle? Who is Paul's only refreshment while facing death? What do we know about him? Well, almost nothing. Talk about a little-known hero! Of all the little people in the Bible, this is one of the least known. You could write all you know about Onesiphorus on the back of a stamp and still have room to doodle. His name occurs in only two places in the Bible—2 Timothy 1 and 2 Timothy 4. That's not much, but it's enough to know that God loves to use little people to do big things.

The Beginning of a Friendship

Little is said about exactly how Paul met Onesiphorus. They probably encountered each other at Ephesus. This was an important city on the west coast of Asia Minor, what is today Turkey. Paul visited there briefly on his second missionary journey and then returned to Ephesus for an extended stay during his third missionary journey.

In its early days, Ephesus was a major seaport city, providing a gateway into the interior of Asia Minor. If trading goods were to move to Colosse, Antioch in Psidia or anywhere else in the interior of the country, they would pass through Ephesus. If you visit the impressive ruins of Ephesus today, you will quickly notice that it is no longer a seaport. Over time, the quest for timber and charcoal plus overgrazing led to massive erosion. As the soil washed into the rivers and streams, it filled the harbor with silt. Where once existed a sheltered gulf and deep waterway, there now is only a marshy plain.

Even in Paul's time, the people of Ephesus could see the handwriting on the wall. Astutely they changed their focus from trade to tourism. Ephesus bragged of a theater that seated an estimated 25,000 people. It was one of the most imposing structures in antiquity. A main thoroughfare 105 feet wide ran from the theater to the harbor with a huge gate at each end. Along each side of the thoroughfare were rows of columns 50 feet deep. Behind the columns were baths, gymnasiums and impressive buildings. It was quite a sight.

But ancient Ephesus' superlative claim to fame was the temple of Artemis, or Diana. "Artemis" was her Greek name; "Diana," her Roman name. She was the daughter of Zeus and the mother goddess of Ephesus. Her temple measured 460 feet by 246 feet and was 66 feet high. Just to give you an idea of its size, the temple was four times larger than the Parthenon on top of the Acropolis in Athens. It was an impressive site, one of the seven wonders of the ancient world.

It is likely that Onesiphorus, as a Gentile, was involved in the worship of Artemis. In the ancient world, the worship of fertility gods and goddesses normally involved sexual immorality. Often the fertility they wanted for their crops and animals was acted out by worshipers with temple priestesses. It was a very sensual place.

For Onesiphorus, however, all that was about to change. When Paul and company arrived in Ephesus proclaiming the Gospel, Onesiphorus saw a better way. He trusted Christ as his Savior, was forgiven of his sins and began a new life in Christ. Imagine his gratitude as he found release from the bondage of depravity. Imagine what freedom he felt when he no longer "worshiped" at the pagan temples. Imagine the gratitude that blossomed into friendship for the one who brought him the good news that his sins could be forgiven forever. Onesiphorus undoubtedly looked for tangible ways to express his appreciation for Paul's ministry to him (2 Tim. 1:18).

There is no friendship like eternal friendship. And no eternal friendship is as deeply felt as the one between you and the person who introduced you to Jesus Christ. While I have not kept in close contact with those I've been used to lead to the Savior, I have always felt a keen kinship with them. And I know many who count me as a dear friend because we are eternally linked in Christ.

The Fusing of a Friendship

The friendship between Paul and Onesiphorus, which was forged in gratitude, was solidified in the heat of persecution. Nothing makes close friendships like shared adversity. "A friend in need is a friend indeed."

Undoubtedly, Paul and Onesiphorus shared a great deal of adversity in Ephesus, as did all the believers there. Here's why. Under the leadership of the apostle Paul, "the word of the Lord grew mightily and prevailed" (Acts 19:20). God's power was demonstrated in amazing ways "so that even handkerchiefs or aprons were brought from his body to the sick, and the diseases left them and the evil spirits went out of them" (v. 12). Events like this "became known both to all Jews and Greeks dwelling in Ephesus; and fear fell on them all, and the name of the Lord Jesus was magnified. And many who had believed came confessing and telling their deeds" (vv. 17-18).

By themselves, these things probably were not sufficient to generate significant persecution. But as proof of their sincerity, many of those who had practiced magic brought their books together and publicly burned them. No big deal? Think about this. When the value of these items was added up, it totaled 50,000 pieces of silver (v. 19). We'd all be on Easy Street if we had 50,000 silver coins.

You can imagine the rejoicing among the Christians. People were changed and the whole city knew it. But what was a cause for rejoicing in the church was a cause for concern to the Ephesians. Remember, Ephesus was a tourist town. Many Ephesians made their living by selling statues, amulets and other trinkets associated with Artemis worship and the occult. Men like Demetrius, the silversmith, who made souvenirs of the temple, began to feel the pinch. Angered by a decline in his business, Demetrius rounded up a mob and complained, "Men, you know that we have our prosperity by this trade. Moreover you see and hear that not only at Ephesus, but throughout almost all Asia, this Paul has persuaded and turned away many people, saying that they are not gods which are made with hands. So not only is this trade of ours in danger of falling into disrepute, but also the temple of the great goddess Diana may be despised and her magnificence destroyed, whom all Asia and the world worship" (vv. 25-27).

Under the double threat of losing their religion and their livelihood, the merchants became greatly agitated. Pouring out of their meeting place, they seized Gaius and Aristarchus, two of Paul's travel companions, and rushed down the wide boulevard that led to the theater. Once there, they held a two-hour pagan pep rally, chanting, "Great is Diana of the Ephesians!" Only the persuasive argument of the town clerk prevented this would-be lynch mob from completing their mission.

While we all know about the adversity Paul and company endured on this occasion, the chances are that Luke, the author of the Book of Acts, did not relate half the trials that came to Paul at Ephesus. Later the apostle shared with the Corinthians that he "fought with beasts at Ephesus" (1 Cor. 15:32). Angry merchants were nothing compared with angry lions. Paul also spoke "of our trouble which came to us in Asia . . . so that we despaired even of life" (2 Cor. 1:8).

Ephesus was the apostle's number-one trouble spot. Yet out of this crucible of trials and tribulations was forged a friendship between Onesiphorus and Paul that would span the years and cross the miles. When Paul's hour of greatest need came, it wasn't the "big" names who were there for him. It was his friend Onesiphorus, short in recognition but long in friendship.

The Testing of a Friendship

Every friendship experiences a time when the ties are tested. Maybe you've had a friend who moved away and your friendship was stretched to its limits. Maybe your friendship has been tested by a serious misunderstanding. "He said, she said" often hampers friendships. That's why dogs have so many friends; they wag their tail instead of their tongue. But it always comes down to the same question: Is your friendship strong enough to withstand the strain of stressful events? When the test of your friendship comes, will you still be friends when it's over?

For Paul, the test of his friendship with Onesiphorus came during his final imprisonment. Rome was filled with intrigue and suspicion. Nero was the emperor and even many Romans questioned his sanity. He engineered a brutal and bloodthirsty persecution of Christians. Innocent believers were sewn up in the skins of wild animals and torn apart by savage dogs. They were thrown to wild animals in the amphitheater. Christians were even dipped in tar, set on fire and used as torches to light Nero's gardens at night. Indescribable and unbelievable cruelty was commonplace. These were dangerous days to be a Christian.

99

It's understandable, then, why Paul said, "all those in Asia have turned away from me." Paul was public enemy number one in Rome. To be associated with a well-known Christian evangelist would have been equivalent to signing your own death sentence. Paul sat in prison; people stayed away from him in droves.

Yet the danger didn't stop Onesiphorus. Paul says that "when he arrived in Rome, he sought me out very diligently and found me" (2 Tim. 1:17). It's obvious that Onesiphorus made a special trip to Rome just to find Paul. When all the other Christians were fleeing the city or keeping a low profile, Onesiphorus stepped up to the plate. He walked right into the hornet's nest for the sake of his friendship with Paul.

But there's more. Onesiphorus spent no little effort in locating his imprisoned friend. There were hundreds of prisons in Rome. In which one would he find Paul? It wouldn't be easy. Because of his notoriety, some speculate that Paul may have been consigned to a private prison rather than one normally used for criminals. Can't you see Onesiphorus making his way in the night from prison to prison searching for his friend? It would take significant commitment and a diligent search to find Paul.

But Paul and Onesiphorus were genuine friends, and true friendship considers neither dangers nor obstacles. Max Lucado tells the story of the soldier in World War I who asked his officer if he might go out into the "no man's land" between the trenches to bring in one of his comrades who lay grievously wounded. "You can go," said the officer, "but it's not worth it. Your friend has probably been killed, and you will throw your own life away." But the man went. Somehow he managed to get to his friend, hoist him onto his shoulder and bring him back to the trenches. The two of them tumbled in together and lay at the bottom of the trench. The officer looked sadly at the would-be rescuer, and then said, "I told you it wouldn't be worth it. Your friend is dead and you are mortally wounded." "It was worth it, though, sir," he said. "How do you mean, 'worth it'? I tell you, your friend is dead." "Yes, sir," the boy answered, "but it was worth it, because when I got to him he was still alive, and he said to me, 'Jim, I knew you'd come.'"

I suspect that when Onesiphorus finally found Paul, the apostle said, "I knew you'd come." That's the kind of friend that Onesiphorus was. He hadn't taken Friendship 101. He hadn't attended any special seminars on "How to Be a Friend." His wasn't the sweet, syrupy friendship that is only skin-deep. His was real friendship. Onesiphorus was no big-name apostle; he was just an ordinary person like you and me. But what he lacked in fame he made up for in friendship.

Lessons From the Little Guy

There are lessons to be learned from this friendship, and almost all of them are taught to us by Onesiphorus. See if your friendships are built on these same principles.

Consistency. Onesiphorus was no fly-by-night friend. He was not there in the good times and absent in the hard times. The friends we make in prosperity we often lose in adversity. But Paul's friendship with Onesiphorus was forged in adversity. Nothing would cool it or deter it now.

Onesiphorus "often refreshed" Paul. I don't know exactly what that means. Maybe he brought cool drinks of water to him and refreshed his tongue. Perhaps he read the Old Testament Scriptures to him and refreshed Paul's spirit. Whatever it means, Onesiphorus did it consistently. He did it often.

Friendships need room to grow, and they will grow if they are consistent. Friendship is not a gift; it is earned every day. Onesiphorus earned Paul's friendship often. Don't your friends deserve this kind of consistency from you?

Initiative. Friendships are active, not passive. The Bible says, "A man who has friends must himself be friendly" (Prov. 18:24). Paul did not call Onesiphorus to come to Rome. The apostle didn't summon him to a ministry of refreshment. It was Onesiphorus' idea; it was his initiative.

Friendships require initiative. You must seek out people to become your friends. And you must seek out your friends when they need you. That's the one thing Job's friends did right. When Job needed someone, his friends came to him, sat with him and wept with him (Job 2:11-13). They took the initiative; so did Onesiphorus.

Paul was worthy of being refreshed by everyone, but only Onesiphorus took the initiative to seek him out. When your friends need you, do you seek them out? When your friend is terminal with cancer, are you afraid you won't know what to say so you stay away? That's the worst possible thing you could do. Take the initiative to be a friend. Seek out your friend in need and be a friend indeed.

Diligence. If you want your friendships to work, work on them. Be diligent in dealing with your friends. Paul said, "When he [Onesiphorus] arrived in Rome, he sought me out very diligently and found me" (2 Tim. 1:17).

I suppose Onesiphorus could have arrived in Rome, checked out a few prisons and returned to Ephesus. He could have offered to the Ephesian believers, "You don't understand. Rome is a very big city. There are a lot of prisons there. I tried to find Paul, I really did. But finally I had to give up."

Have you ever been a part of your church visitation team? You go out knocking on doors, inviting people to come to church. Have you noticed how timid you can be? You knock on the door once, twice, and then you say, "Oh, well. It looks like nobody's home. Let's get outta here." Or you call people on the phone to invite them to church. You're a bit timid so you let the phone ring once, twice, and quickly say, "I guess no one is going to answer." So you hang up and think, *Whew! That was close.*

Onesiphorus was diligent in looking for Paul. In fact, he was so diligent he wouldn't give up until he found him. His friendship was too important to him just to give it the old college try. He wouldn't stop at anything short of success. He was diligent in nurturing their friendship.

Interesting, isn't it, that some of the biggest lessons in life are learned from some of the littlest people in the Bible? Onesiphorus is one of them. We know very little about him. He is mentioned in only one epistle—2 Timothy. He was not an apostle, not an elder, not a preacher, not even a deacon. He was just an ordinary guy with an extraordinary appreciation of fine friendships.

The next time your friend needs you, needs some refreshment, needs someone just to be there, be an Onesiphorus. Be there. Be consistent. Be diligent. Be a friend. "A friend loves at all times, and a brother is born for adversity" (Prov. 17:17). Paul's prison was primitive and plain; it was dark and damp. The only ornamentation his prison had was the friendship of Onesiphorus. Hang some ornaments in your friend's house today. That's something that anyone can do, even little people like you and me.

MICAIAH

Name:	**Micaiah**
Nationality:	Jew
Era:	Circa 900 B.C.
Location:	Samaria
Reference:	1 Kings 22:7-28; 2 Chronicles 18:6-27

Most Memorable Accomplishment:

Ahab, king of Israel, invited Jehoshaphat, king of Judah, to join him in battle against Assyria. Jehoshaphat agreed but suggested that they should first inquire of the Lord concerning their chances of success. Immediately Ahab assembled 400 prophets at the city gate of Samaria. Unanimously they encouraged the kings to fight, assuring them of victory. Jehoshaphat, however, asked, "Is there not still a prophet of the LORD here, that we may inquire of Him?" Ahab reluctantly answered, "There is still one man, Micaiah the son of Imlah, by whom we may inquire of the LORD; but I hate him, because he does not prophesy good concerning me, but evil" (1 Kings 22:7-8). Micaiah always told the king what God wanted him to hear, but since Ahab lived so wickedly it was never what he wanted to hear. He was the prophet you loved to hate.

CHAPTER 10

Micaiah

The Prophet
You Love to Hate

The Old Testament is an astonishing book. Too many pastors and preachers avoid it or only occasionally include it in their preaching. That's lamentable because the history of Israel reads like a modern spy novel. There's mystery and intrigue, love and war, dysfunctional families, plot and counterplot. It's got a little of everything. Unfortunately, some of the greatest characters in the Old Testament have escaped our notice. One of them is Micaiah. This is his story.

Micaiah was the prophet you loved to hate, at least King Ahab did. Israel's king despised Micaiah because, as Ahab said in his own words, "he does not prophesy good concerning me, but evil" (1 Kings 22:8). It's not easy to love someone who is always talking about your shortcomings, but Micaiah did much more than that. He actually had the backbone to stick by the truth when all the paid prophets of the king told Ahab only what he wanted to hear.

Living With an Unhealthy Alliance

The year was 853 B.C. It was one of those extraordinary periods in history. Ever since the ten tribes of Israel seceded from Judah in 931 B.C., there had been little friendly contact between the two kingdoms. Indeed, there was open warfare between them. First Kings 15:6 says, "And there was war between Rehoboam [Judah] and Jeroboam [Israel] all the days of his life."

But this year was one of those unique periods of history between wars. There haven't been many of them. Nobody in the

Middle East was fighting with anybody. The first verse of 1 Kings 22 says, "Now three years passed without war between Syria and Israel." But this was just the calm before the storm.

In a very unusual gesture, Jehoshaphat, the king of Judah, paid a visit to Ahab, the king of Israel, at his palace in Samaria. That in itself is remarkable. Ahab was one of the worst kings Israel ever had; Jehoshaphat was one of the best Judah ever had. You might expect this would put the two kings on a collision course, but it didn't.

If you dig into the family tree, you find that Jehoram, the son of Jehoshaphat, had married Athaliah, the daughter of Ahab. That meant these two kings shared grandchildren, and all of us who are grandparents know what that means. But one set of grandparents was evil, and the other was godly—a time bomb waiting to explode.

In the course of this little outing, Ahab mentioned to Jehoshaphat that he would like to have back Ramoth in Gilead, one of the towns he had lost earlier to the Syrians. Ramoth was one of the chief cities of the tribe of Gad, 28 miles east of the Jordan River.

Imagine you were sitting in Ahab's ivory palace that day. The conversation you would have overheard must have gone something like this:

"My dear friend Jehoshaphat," Ahab said, "did you know that the Syrians are still holding Ramoth in Gilead? It's important that we get it back, but I don't think we can take it by ourselves. Would you consider joining us in battle?"

Now there's a switch—Israel and Judah fighting side by side instead of fighting each other. Right here is where the king of Judah should have ended his visit and gone back home, but he didn't.

"Count me in," Jehoshaphat replied. "All my troops and my cavalry will join you."

Jehoshaphat was a man of God. One of the five great revivals among God's people in the Old Testament occurred during his reign. He had a genuine heart for Jehovah, but this unholy alliance could never be blessed by God. Even though it was a Jew helping a fellow Jew against a pagan neighbor, Ahab was more pagan than any Syrian.

Living Under the Shadow of Another

Into this precarious situation came one of God's little people. His name was Micaiah, a prophet you may never have heard of, but the prophet King Ahab loved to hate.

One of the reasons you may be unfamiliar with Micaiah is that he was a contemporary of Elijah. When we read 1 and 2 Kings we often focus on events in the life of Elijah—and for good reason. He was the great prophet, dominating the prophetic revelation to Israel during this period. His story eclipses all others in this portion of Scripture.

It was Elijah who called for a three-year drought that crippled Israel and brought Ahab to his knees (1 Kings 17:1). It was Elijah who engaged in that legendary contest with the prophets of Baal on Mount Carmel (1 Kings 18:19-40). It was Elijah who wrapped his mantle together and struck the waters of the Jordan River so Elisha and he could pass over on dry ground (2 Kings 2:8). It's easy to see why Elijah was the dominant prophet of the time, a powerful spokesman for God.

Often when a person of God dominates his period of history, we fail to notice others who are doing equally valuable work for God. Elijah himself made that mistake. He complained to God, "I have been very zealous for the LORD God of hosts; for the children of Israel have forsaken Your covenant, torn down Your altars, and killed Your prophets with the sword. I alone am left; and they seek to take my life" (1 Kings 19:10). God gently reminded Elijah He had 7,000 others who had not bowed to Baal (v. 18), and one of them was Micaiah.

Micaiah lived in the shadow of the giant Elijah. Not many know his name or what he did, but he was just as important to God as Elijah. He did what God asked, and that's all God expects of any of us. He doesn't expect us to be Elijah or the apostle Paul or D. L. Moody or Billy Graham. He expects us to be us, but obedient to Him. What God gives you to do is just as important as what He gives others to do, but only if you do it. Like Micaiah, you may live in the shadow of a superstar, but those who live in the shadows rarely are afflicted with the "I alone am left" disease.

Living With Unpopular Truth

When Jehoshaphat agreed to join Ahab's invasion of Gilead, he made one important stipulation. Jehoshaphat said, "Please inquire for the word of the LORD today" (22:5). The king of Judah had enough spiritual discernment to know that regardless of the strength of their armies, the battle was futile if the Lord wasn't in it. He wanted a prophet to ask God if Israel and Judah should go off to war.

Ahab's response was typical. He summoned 400 prophets of the Lord to ask if they should fight. These were likely prophets of Jehovah from all outward appearances, or Jehoshaphat would not have accepted them. Nevertheless, they were on Ahab's payroll. He had them in his back pocket. Their job was to tell Ahab whatever he wanted to hear. That happens often today, and not just in government.

The easiest way to become popular today is to find out what the people want and give it to them. Much of talk radio and television is built on this premise. Find a topic that everybody has an opinion about and let them share it. Decide what people want to hear about and then tell them what they want to hear. Be sympathetic. Be relational. Be sincere. But whatever you do, don't be a prophet. Prophets frequently had to deliver bad news, and Christians today don't like prophetic preaching any more than the Israelites did. Get your topic from the people, not from God, and you'll have the people eating out of your hands.

I'm afraid Paul's warning has come true. People want to hear "their own desires, because they have itching ears" (2 Tim. 4:3). They will flock to hear those who say what pleases them, but they have no time to listen to the voice of God. Ahab's paid preachers told him to go into battle, for the Lord would give him victory. They were sensitive to Ahab's desires, but Ahab's greatest need was truth.

Fortunately, Jehoshaphat had enough spiritual discernment to know that these guys hadn't heard from God in ages, so he asked Ahab, "Is there not still a prophet of the LORD here, that we may inquire of Him?" (v. 7). Ahab's response was classic. In essence he said, "Well, yes, there is this Micaiah, but he doesn't demonstrate any desire to please me. He only speaks the truth. I hate him for it" (v. 8).

All Micaiah did was tell Ahab what God told him to say. All he did was tell the king what he needed to hear. All Micaiah did was tell Ahab the truth, but truth-tellers are never popular in a sinful society. They weren't then; they aren't now.

Living As a Presumed Failure

Have you ever lived as a failure? Oh, you weren't a failure, of course, but everybody thought you were. Things just didn't go your way. Others did what you did and had great success. They got noticed. They were called by the local TV news for an interview. You did what God asked you to do and lived in poverty and obscurity the whole time. It can be a bit depressing.

Micaiah was like that. Not only did he live under the shadow of Elijah, but he also lived a good deal of the time in prison. When brought before the two kings and asked if they should try to recapture Ramoth, Micaiah proved he was the master of sarcasm. He responded facetiously, "Go and prosper, for the LORD will deliver it into the hand of the king!" (v. 15).

Ahab knew Micaiah was putting him on. He replied, "How many times have I told you to tell me only what the Lord spoke to you?" To that Micaiah could have said, "None." This was Ahab's attempt to impress Jehoshaphat. So Micaiah dropped the jesting. He spoke a parable. Jesus did the same thing. When people rejected the plain truth of His message, He communicated that truth in a parable, a picture story that taught the same truth.

Micaiah's parable spoke of Israel as sheep wandering aimlessly on the mountains because their shepherd had disappeared. They all returned home in peace even though they had no one to lead them.

Ahab was no dummy. He knew he was the shepherd in the parable and that if he went to war with the Syrians, his soldiers would return home in peace, but without him. The king was livid. Angrily he complained to Jehoshaphat, "Did I not tell you that he would not prophesy good concerning me, but evil?" (v. 18).

Ahab wanted to lash out at Micaiah. He turned to his royal guard and commanded, "Put this fellow in prison and feed him with bread of affliction and water of affliction, until I come in peace" (v. 27).

This was much more than the king's "So there!" It was his way of punishing Micaiah for telling the truth.

Ahab believed when he returned from battle in one piece that all Israel would know that Micaiah, the prophet he loved to hate, was a liar. But it was not to be. Micaiah was anything but a failure, as the rest of the story demonstrates. Besides, those who fail are really only failures if they fail God. Micaiah didn't, but Ahab certainly did.

Living With the Consequences

Ahab and Jehoshaphat joined forces against the Syrians. The wily Ahab convinced Jehoshaphat that it would be better if only one of them wore their royal garments into battle and, of course, he deferred to Jehoshaphat. But it was a trick. Dressed this way, Jehoshaphat became the target of every enemy arrow while Ahab, dressed in a private's uniform, would escape.

Ahab rejected the only prophet who would tell him the truth and he suffered the consequences. In the heat of battle, one of the Syrian soldiers decided to empty his quiver so his captain wouldn't think he had sluffed off. He put the arrow on his bow, pulled the string and let the arrow fly aimlessly into the air in the general direction of the Israelites. If anyone ever doubted the sovereignty of God, they shouldn't after what happened next.

The arrow indeed found the army of Israel. In fact, it found one soldier dressed in a private's uniform. Of all the soldiers of Israel, this aimless arrow drew a bead on Ahab. Still, the king was clad in the armor of an infantryman. Surely that arrow couldn't pierce his armor, and it didn't. God not only guided the arrow to Ahab, but He guided the tip of that arrow between the joints of his armor, and Ahab died (v. 34). Ahab lived and died with the consequences of his sin.

And what about our man Micaiah? Instead of being proven a false prophet, he was vindicated for taking a stand for the truth.

What does this little-known hero teach us? For one thing, he reminds us that you don't have to be the senior pastor to minister to your people. You don't have to be the most popular teacher to teach your class. You don't have to have the name that everybody remembers to have your name remembered by God. You don't have to please everybody; you just have to please God.

Micaiah lived in Elijah's shadow all his life. But when it came to prophesying the death of wicked King Ahab, that fell to one of God's little people. You don't have to be a big-time player to get the job done. Micaiah is a brilliant example of one of God's little people. He wasn't a star, but he was faithful. He did what God told him to do.

So what does God have in mind for you? Playing second fiddle doesn't mean you're not in the orchestra. If there were only a first chair, it wouldn't be an orchestra anyway; it would be a solo. God needs Elijahs, and I thank Him for people like that famous prophet. But God also needs Micaiahs, people like you and me. We have a place in God's plan, too, if we are willing to obey Him. That's the key—obedience, a willingness to do whatever God asks and not worry about who's watching us.

But there's another lesson to be learned from Micaiah. He wasn't a household name (except in Ahab's household), but he had the courage to tell the truth and take a stand when it was needed. Did you notice Ahab's response when Jehoshaphat asked if there was anybody who was still a prophet of the Lord? He said, "There is still one man" (v. 8). One man. It doesn't take many when there is one who is willing to obey. Will you be that one?

The next time the school board meets to fire a Christian teacher who presents God's story of creation as an alternative to the theory of evolution, you don't have to be a renowned scientist to speak your piece. Just speak the truth. The next time there is a bill before your legislature that expands the law legalizing the killing of innocent babies in their mother's womb, you don't have to be the Surgeon General to stand up against it. Just tell them what God says.

God's heroes aren't always the Elijahs of this world. Sometimes they're the Micaiahs. Sometimes they're the little people—people just like you and me. So if you haven't called down fire from heaven lately or parted the waters of the Jordan, relax. God doesn't want you to do that. Find out what He wants you to do, and do it. That's being God's hero.

ASAHEL

Name:	**Asahel**
Nationality:	Jew
Era:	Circa 1004 B.C.
Location:	The Wilderness of Gibeon
Reference:	2 Samuel 2:18-33; 2 Chronicles 17:8

Most Memorable Accomplishment:

Although he did not get his man, Asahel showed tremendous courage and determination in pursuing him. Abner, the captain of Saul's army, and his troops were beaten by David's men in a particularly bitter battle. When Abner managed to escape, Asahel determined to pursue him. As he did, Abner identified his pursuer because of Asahel's unusual speed and running ability. Abner knew he could not outrun the valiant soldier, so he attempted to intimidate and threaten him. But Asahel wouldn't give up. Finally, Abner turned and challenged Asahel, killing the fleet-footed hero with a spear.

CHAPTER 11

Asahel

Fleet of Foot

Their names thrive in the memories of millions. Who can forget their achievements? They are among the fastest men ever to run on the earth. At one time or another, they set world records for pushing themselves to the limit while rocketing down the track. Men like Michael Johnson, Donovan Bailey and Carl Lewis distinguished themselves by their speed. They were proven champions, perennially unbeatable and perpetually in the headlines.

But these were all latecomers. Others fleet of foot have preceded them. Who can forget Bob Hayes, track star of the 1960s turned wide receiver for the Dallas Cowboys? All you had to do was throw him the ball and watch him spring free from everybody on his dash into the end zone. And before him were others, equally outstanding, equally speedy.

Perhaps you remember the acclaimed film *Chariots of Fire.* It was the story of Eric Liddell, who, as a young man, discovered that he could run fast for the glory of God. And run fast he did. Yet his strict Scottish religious instruction taught him to honor God above athletics. Later in life he became a missionary to China and was held as a prisoner of war. Even under duress, he continued his personal pursuit of God until his death at the Weishien concentration camp in 1945.

Yet champions are just ordinary people through whom God does extraordinary things for His glory. They are little people who serve a big God. Wouldn't you love to see one of those computer simulations that pits a champion of the past against a champion of the present? I think the champion whose story is highlighted in this chapter could hold his own against Donovan Bailey or Michael Johnson, and yet it's likely you don't even know his name.

Third-string Brother

Do you have any brothers or sisters? Are any of them famous? It's not easy being the sibling of a famous person. Just ask Andrew. He is mentioned 12 times in the New Testament, half of those times as "Simon Peter's brother." He went through life as "What's his name—you know, Peter's brother," and that can be tough. But there's something even worse. How would you like to be a third-string brother, kid brother to two famous older brothers? That was Asahel's problem. Still, he overcame his anonymity to accomplish a great feat for God.

Four men recorded in the Old Testament bore the name Asahel. One was a Levite sent by King Jehoshaphat to teach the Law to the people (2 Chron. 17:8). Another Levite by that name was appointed by King Hezekiah as an overseer of the temple offerings (2 Chron. 17:8). Another, the father of Jonathan, helped Ezra deal with those who had married pagan women during the Captivity (Ezra 10:15). But Asahel the fleet of foot, while not well-known himself, was a member of a very prominent family in Israel.

Being an unknown is bad enough, but being an unknown in a famous family is even worse. Asahel was the son of Zeruiah, David's half-sister. That meant he could call the king of Israel "Uncle Dave" (although he probably didn't). Imagine what it must have been like to be kin to the king. Likely he had access to the palace as a young boy and enjoyed all the contests of the Jerusalem games. What boy wouldn't visit the palace often if his uncle were king?

But if Asahel was to get any notice from the king, he had two obstacles to overcome. They were named Joab and Abishai, his older brothers. If you put your head closer to the page and listen carefully, you can almost hear them. Joab and Abishai are planning to spend the day in the palace gym and they whine to Zerulah, "Mom, do we have to take Asahel with us? He's too little.

116

He'll only slow us down." But the day would come when Asahel would become famous for his speed, and his brothers would rue that day the rest of their lives.

Asahel lived in the shadow of his brothers. When David was on the run from King Saul, twice the shepherd prince had opportunity to kill the man who wanted to kill him, but he did not. The first time, Saul was in the cave at En Gedi   (1 Sam. 24). The second time, Saul and his army were asleep near the hill of Hachilah. David said to Abishai and Ahimelech the Hittite, "Who will go down with me to Saul in the camp?" (26:6). Obviously this was extremely dangerous, but without hesitation Abishai said, "I will go down with you." When David and Abishai crept into the camp of the king, Abishai was eager to kill Saul. David's intent, however, was not to murder his enemy but to protect him. He took Saul's spear and his jug of water and they slipped out of the camp unnoticed. Then David called to Abner, Saul's captain and the most valiant man in Israel, and asked him why he hadn't protected the king adequately. David and Abishai humiliated Abner. It was a daring move. Everyone in Israel knew of David and Abishai's bravery. How could young Asahel live up to that?

And as much as he lived in the shadow of Abishai, he was even further in the recesses of big brother Joab's silhouette. Joab was the commander of David's troops, the top general of the army. He was a man's man. He was fearless and at times ruthless. He had the savvy to advise the king on repeatedly successful military strategy. He also had such a rapport with David that he felt at liberty to question the king's actions (1 Chron. 21:3). The bravery and military prowess of Joab were legendary. Little Asahel could look up to his older brother, but he could never look past him.

And what's more, the only thing worse than being kid brother to two heroes is being kid brother to two heroes working together. How would you handle being the younger brother of two men who fought together and around whom the ballads and war stories grew, but you were left out?

When Hanun, king of Ammon, humiliated David's men by shaving their beards, Joab and Abishai sprang into action (1 Chron. 19). Joab and his armies took on the Syrians, who had joined the fray, and Abishai and his armies took on the Ammonites. They invited King David to mop up what was left of the enemy, so he would be credited with the victory. What a team these brothers were. They were better than the Kennedy brothers in American politics or the Baldwin brothers in American films. Let's face it; it's hard for a little brother to match sibling exploits like these.

Living in the shadows is no fun, but it is safe. Sometimes when we try to escape the shadow of others, we find the sunlight of responsibility far more dangerous than the shadow of anonymity. Asahel would learn this lesson in tragedy.

Rise to Prominence

This does not imply that Asahel had no exploits of his own, but his bravery was often overshadowed by that of his brothers. Asahel, whose name means "God is doer," wanted to be a doer as well. He wanted to make a difference, do something memorable, accomplish the impossible. He made himself available to Uncle David for whatever the king wanted. And then the day came when he was lifted from the shadow of his brothers.

Apparently, King David changed the guard attached to the palace at Jerusalem on a monthly basis. First Chronicles 27:1 says, "And the children of Israel, according to their number, the heads of fathers' houses, the captains of thousands and hundreds and their officers, served the king in every matter of the military divisions. These divisions came in and went out month by month throughout all the months of the year, each division having twenty-four thousand." For a full month, a contingent of soldiers would serve David in Jerusalem and then be sent elsewhere in the kingdom to serve the other 11 months.

Each division of soldiers consisted of 24,000 and thus represented a significant fighting force. It would take a talented and dedicated captain to lead these men—and each division was headed by such a man.

Jashobeam, one of David's three mightiest warriors (1 Chron. 11:11), headed the first infantry division. They were to serve David the first month of the year, corresponding to our April. Other commanders were equally well known. Benaiah led the Cherethite and Pelethite division (18:17). He was a man who "had killed two lion-like heroes of Moab" and "went down and killed a lion in the midst of a pit on a snowy day" (2 Sam. 23:20). He even had a hand in insuring that Solomon was crowned king after David's death (1 Kings 1).

Asahel finally came into his own when he found himself in the company of such legendary fighting men. He was named as the fourth captain, whose men would serve David during the fourth month of the year. That meant that during the hot months of the summer, when other divisions were stationed in the wilderness and along the frontier, Asahel and his men pulled Jerusalem duty in the high mountains of Judea. Not a bad assignment.

Things were finally starting to go Asahel's way. He was the leader of 24,000 soldiers. He was one of only 12 men entrusted to this sacred duty. He could serve his uncle with pride and distinction. It is evident that he had climbed out of his brothers' shadows, at least to some degree.

But young Asahel was also part of a more distinguished group than this. He was a member of David's elite band known as the "mighty men" or "the thirty." This may have been just a technical term for David's select soldiers, since both 2 Samuel 23 and 1 Chronicles 11 mention more than 30 men. Or perhaps the number remained at 30, with some men replacing others as they were killed in battle (e.g., Uriah the Hittite). In either case, these were David's elite guard, the supreme fighting machine of Israel. And in both passages where their names are given, guess who is near the top of the list? Welcome to the big leagues, Asahel.

Fall to Zeal

In spite of his choice assigment, Asahel's name is barely remembered today. He is one of the little people who served a big God. He had tremendous zeal for God and for Israel, and for his Uncle David. But zeal by itself is always insufficient to make us useful servants of God. The story of Asahel is the perfect example. He not only rose to prominence, but he fell to zeal without wisdom.

Asahel does not come to our attention because of his family ties. He was not distinguished because he was one of only 12 leaders chosen to serve the king. He did not leave his mark as one of David's mighty men. No, Asahel's claim to fame was his speed. He could lead, but he could also run. He was brave, but oh, how he could run. Asahel was renowned for his fleetness of foot, but sometimes God's heroes can be too fast.

After the death of Saul, one of Saul's sons, Ishbosheth, was made king over Gilead, Ephraim and all Israel (2 Sam. 2:8-9). This was an attempt to keep David from becoming king of Israel as well as Judah. While Ishbosheth was crowned king, Abner, Saul's brilliant military general, was the real power behind the throne. Abner was extremely loyal to Saul, which made him extremely dangerous to David.

Abner and his counterpart, Joab, were constantly involved in a political game of cat and mouse, but it couldn't continue. Something had to be done. Israel's general and Judah's general scheduled a high-level meeting at the pool of Gibeon. Abner sat on one side of the pool; Joab sat on the other. They decided to settle their differences with surrogate soldiers. Each side would chose 12 of their premier fighting men to duke it out on behalf of Israel and Judah. Whoever was left standing would win the war for their side.

Sounds like a pretty risky scheme, and it was. In fact, Saul's dozen killed David's dozen while simultaneously being killed themselves. All 24 fell dead on the battlefield. Nothing was gained except to stir up additional hatred.

What followed was the arena that brought Asahel to his greatest prominence. A great battle ensued in which Joab and the forces of Judah were victorious. Abner was beaten and fled. Present at the conflict were the three brothers—Joab, Abishai and Asahel. Second Samuel 2:18 makes special note of Asahel's outstanding speed: "And Asahel was as fleet of foot as a wild gazelle." Even though Abner had a head start, Asahel broke rank with his brothers and ran after him. They couldn't call him back; they couldn't catch him.

Asahel wanted so much to be used of God. He wanted so much to serve his king valiantly. And, likely, he wanted so much to distinguish himself from his legendary brothers. Asahel not only ran after Abner, but he pursued him doggedly. "And in going he did not turn to the right hand or to the left" (v. l9). He was zealous, he was dedicated, he was determined, but he wasn't very wise.

Abner heard the footsteps of a faster runner closing in on him. Who could it be? Who could run so fast that he could catch the mighty warrior? It had to be Asahel. "Then Abner looked behind him, and said, 'Are you Asahel?' And he answered, 'I am'" (v. 20). Asahel was an idealist; Abner, a realist. Asahel could run very fast, faster than anyone. But Abner was the premier fighter in Israel and Judah. Asahel was no match for Abner, and Abner knew it.

You have to admire what Saul's general did next. He pleaded with Asahel. "Turn aside to your right hand or to your left, and lay hold on one of the young men and take his armor for yourself" (v. 21). Abner begged Asahel to stop pursuing him, not because he was afraid Asahel would catch him, but because he knew what would happen when Asahel did. He implored Asahel to stop long enough to put on some armor for protection against the mighty spear of Abner. Asahel refused. He never considered what he would do if he caught Abner. He just ran, because running was what he did best.

Again Abner pleaded with him. He knew if they fought, Asahel would lose and Abner would shame himself before Asahel's greater brother, Joab. Abner was not afraid of Joab (and certainly not afraid of Asahel), but he was a man of honor. He didn't want to have to kill Asahel, but 2 Samuel 2:23 records the tragic results: "However, he refused to turn aside. Therefore Abner struck him in the stomach with the blunt end of the spear, so that the spear came out of his back; and he fell down there

121

and died on the spot. So it was that as many as came to the place where Asahel fell down and died, stood still."

Although everyone respected Asahel's zeal—so much so that they always stopped at that site to pay him tribute—the result of his zeal was tragic. Asahel was dead. He died valiantly, but he died foolishly. His death precipitated a blood feud between Abner and Asahel's famous brothers. Immediately Joab began to plot the assassination of Abner.

Eventually the day came when Abner and David, who were bigger men than all the others, attempted to make peace between themselves. Abner knew David was God's choice, so he came to David to deliver the kingdom of Saul to him. Although Abner and David reconciled, the jealous Joab could not. He surreptitiously called Abner aside for private consultation and then treacherously murdered him, stabbing him under the fifth rib, exactly as Abner had done to Asahel (2 Sam. 3:27). That act of betrayal set David and his nephew on a collision course.

Heat and Light

Track-and-field events are usually very close competitions. Records are broken by microseconds. The athletes train long and hard and are very zealous to win. Track-and-field contenders are among the most competitive people alive; that's one of the reasons we admire them. It's why we admire Asahel. He was fleet of foot, perhaps the fastest man alive at the time.

Asahel was one of God's little heroes. What he did, he did for the honor of God. He did it in the service of his uncle-king. He did it for the name of his family. That's very commendable. Asahel was highly motivated and driven by zeal. But even God's heroes can teach us things we shouldn't do if we want to serve the Lord well. What we learn from Asahel is that zeal without wisdom is tragedy.

We all have seen Christians who have misguided zeal for the Lord. They buttonhole everyone they see, stuff a tract in their hand and somewhat angrily announce, "Without Jesus Christ you're on your way to hell!" We cannot have anything but admiration for their zeal. We cannot deny the truth of their words. But they are like Asahel. They lack wisdom, not zeal or truth.

A match produces heat, but it also produces light. The spark that began at an empty tomb in Jerusalem has been fanned into a blaze covering the world. The fire of evangelism gives off both heat and light. If we settle for heat only, we may discharge our responsibility but not lovingly as Jesus did. If we settle for light only, we may win the argument but lose the soul. To deliver the message effectively and see people saved, we need both heat and light.

Asahel was a hero, but a hero filled with heat and no light. He was outgunned right from the start. He was no match for Abner, but the only one who recognized that was Abner. I want to be used of God, as Asahel wanted to be used, and so do you. The best way for God to use us is for us to rely on His strength, not our swiftness. Sometimes we run so fast that we run ahead of God. Let's remember Asahel for his fleetness of foot and be like him in that regard. Let's also remember that his speed was not tempered with the wisdom of God, and not be like him in that way.

God's little people are used in big ways when they take what they have and give it to God, asking Him to bless it. They are not used in big ways when they attempt to accomplish big things for God on their own. Asahel is a wonderful reminder that we should never go into battle without our armor. So before you go chasing after God's enemy, "put on the whole armor of God, that you may be able to stand against the wiles of the devil" (Eph. 6:11). We value the life of Asahel, one of God's little people, if for no other reason than impressing us with this reminder.

JASHOBEAM

Name:	**Jashobeam**
Nationality:	Hachmonite
Era:	Circa 1003 B.C.
Location:	Adullam
Reference:	1 Chronicles 11:11, 15-19

Most Memorable Accomplishment:

David was used to accepting challenges, and so when he gave one, he must have wondered if anyone would rise to it. While hiding out at the cave of Adullam, almost matter-of-factly he sighed, "Oh, that someone would give me a drink of water from the well of Bethlehem" (1 Chron. 11:17). Three of David's "mighty men" were up to the challenge, and Jashobeam was the chief of them. They broke through the Philistine ranks, retrieved the water and fought their way back to Adullam. Though it seemed like an impossible mission, it was not too great of a challenge for these three—Abishai, the brother of Joab, Eleazar, the son of Dodo, and Jashobeam the Hachmonite.

CHAPTER 12

Jashobeam

Chief of Captains

It was a routine day, nothing out of the ordinary. Just another day with the sheep. This was his life.

The young shepherd boy named Abed had no idea when he left the sheepfold that morning that this day would be anything but ordinary. Today would bring an excitement to shepherding he had never known before.

Abed was 15, second-oldest son of his father. They lived near Jericho. Today he would take his sheep, about two dozen or so, up into the hill country. It would be fun. There were lots of caves to explore while the sheep were grazing. He left before sunrise amid the tinkling of the bells hung around the necks of the sheep.

Within hours shepherd and sheep were settled into a cozy little spot where he could look down on the oasis of Jericho. The sheep found some fresh grass and seemed to be content. Abed began to nose around and suddenly felt a wisp of cool air mixing with the air warmed by the Judean sun. *Where could that air be coming from?* It was under him, under the rock he was sitting on. There, through a small crevice, he felt it again.

It was strange. He had been in the area many times before but had never noticed this. Moving the rock ever so slightly, Abed was able to see down into a black hole. It looked like a tiny cave, narrow but apparently quite deep. With boyish wonder, but without caution, Abed reached into the hole. Almost immediately he touched something. *A parchment or a scroll*, he thought. Sure enough, when he pulled it from its dark tomb, it was a scroll. The script was of an old type, but Abed could understand it. It was an ancient journal or something. Maybe a diary. Abed slouched between two rocks and began to read.

It was the record of Jashobeam, chief of captains.

"Today I served my master well. Today he honored me by honoring God. I risked my life for David, and he expressed his devotion to God by giving the fruit of my labors to the Lord. If I live to be 100, I will never live another day like this one. I am most richly blessed."

Abed was puzzled. What could this mean? Who was this Jashobeam, and was it really King David he was talking about? He couldn't wait to get home and ask his uncle, Nibshan. He knew everything.

Later that night Nibshan helped Abed understand what be had read. Indeed, there was a man in ancient Israel by the name of Jashobeam, and he was a servant of David. Abed was eager to get all the facts. Here's what Nibshan knew about it.

The Three Mightiest

In olden times, David, the shepherd boy who killed the great Goliath, was driven from the palace by the jealousy of King Saul. David took refuge in the cave of Adullam, southeast of Jerusalem, out in the middle of nowhere. There, David assembled his own army to defend himself against Saul. These were not highly trained soldiers. In fact, 1 Samuel 22:2 says, "And everyone who was in distress, everyone who was in debt, and everyone who was discontented gathered to him. So he became captain over them. And there were about four hundred men with him." David's army consisted of the homeless, the penniless, the jobless. But they all saw in David a man of God, and they wanted to be on his team.

Through time David's army grew and became better trained and organized. He even had an elite corps of 30 men he called his "mighty men." They were daring and brave. They would do anything for David. Their names are listed in 2 Samuel 23 and 1 Chronicles 11. At the head of the list is Jashobeam, the man young Abed had read about.

Uncle Nibshan could understand why Abed might be confused about Jashobeam's name. It is listed several different ways in the Bible. First Chronicles 11:11 calls him "Jashobeam the son of a Hachmonite" and says that on one occasion he killed 300 of the enemy with a spear. First Chronicles 27:2 further identifies him as the son of Zabdiel and leader of the first division of 24,000 troops, who served and protected David in the palace at Jerusalem. But the writer of 2 Samuel calls him a Tachmonite and gives the alternative name Adino the Eznite (23:8). Apparently this was something of a nickname given to him when he slew 800 soldiers at one time with his spear (not necessarily the same event found in 1 Chronicles 11).

The name everybody knew him by, however, including David, was Jashobeam. That's also the name by which he signed the scroll Abed found. But let's get back to Uncle Nibshan's story of who Jashobeam was.

Chief of All

To be a member of the mighty men was a great honor, not to mention an outstanding achievement. At any given time, only about 30 warriors were part of this celebrated group. There was Eliphelet the son of Ahasbai, and Uriah the Hittite, and Zalmon the Ahohite, but nobody stood out like "the three." They were head and shoulders above the rest.

While the three were included among the mighty men, they were clearly distinct as well. David entrusted more special missions to them than to anyone. He knew he could trust them. They always got the job done, no matter what. The chief of the 30, the creme de la creme, the upper echelon of the mighty men, were these three:

1. Jashobeam, the chief of the chief, was the mightiest of them all.

2. Eleazar, the son of Dodo the Ahohite, was one of David's warriors who defied the Philistines.

3. Shammah, the son of Agee the Hararite, distinguished

himself by single-handedly holding a lentil field against the Philistines when all others fled.

David's army was divided into ranks. First Kings 9:22 mentions several divisions of the men of war: the "officers" (Heb. *sar*) or chiefs of various divisions; the "captains" (Heb. *shaliysh*, which literally means "third"), denoting the man in the chariot crew who rode along to command the battle; the "commanders" (a second man in the chariot who was the fighter); and the cavalry. Jashobeam was a *shaliysh* or captain. In fact, he was the head *shaliysh*. He was the chief of the chief.

As is the case in an army, there are good soldiers and bad soldiers. Among the good are those who distinguish themselves by valor. They become the Green Berets, the Navy Seals, the Rangers. They were David's mighty men. And at the top of the best are the best of the best, the three. And at the top of the three there was Jashobeam.

Servant to David

Nibshan could see Abed was getting restless. A 15-year-old shepherd boy wants to hear stories of battles, not lessons in Hebrew. So the uncle put his arm around the shoulder of his nephew and said, "You must be wondering what is the meaning of this scroll you found. How did Jashobeam risk his life for David? It's a story all the old men of the village know very well, and I want to tell it to you."

Then his uncle went to the back of the house and brought out something wrapped in richly embroidered cloth. As he unwrapped it, Abed could see that it was their family Bible. Nibshan turned to 1 Chronicles 11 and read the story to his young friend.

One day David was hiding out in the cave of Adullam, the one where he gathered his army in the beginning. The Philistines were garrisoned nearby in David's home village, Bethlehem. David was weary of war, but he knew the fight must go on. God had anointed him to be king over Israel, and the Philistines were the mortal enemy of God's people.

David must have been thinking back to more carefree days. Not far from here was where he tended sheep as a boy. He remembered how good it was growing up in Bethlehem. He remembered his young friends. He remembered sitting under the stars at night and wondering about the God who made them. He even composed some songs in praise of God.

While engaged in reflective wonder, David whispered, "Oh, that someone would give me a drink of water from the well of Bethlehem, which is by the gate!" (1 Chron. 11:17). David wasn't really asking for a drink. He had water in his jug. There was also a spring near the cave. It wasn't water he craved; it was Bethlehem, his boyhood home.

Jashobeam was nearby. He overheard David wish for a drink from Bethlehem's well. Eleazar and Shammah heard it too. They got their heads together. "If David wants water from the well of Bethlehem near the gate," they agreed, "then David shall have water from the well."

The fearless three immediately set out for Bethlehem. Since the Philistines were garrisoned there, they knew it wouldn't be easy. But they would do anything for their king.

They battled their way through the enemy lines that encircled the town and made their way to the gate. Philistines were everywhere. Soldiers were sitting on the well, leaning against it, drinking from it. Jashobeam and company were determined to get the water they came for. Eleazar and Shammah continued to fight off the Philistines while Jashobeam drew water from the well. "I've got it!" Jashobeam cried. "Now let's get out of here." As quickly as they came, they were gone.

Jashobeam and his intrepid comrades had to take the long way back to the cave of Adullam. They didn't want to reveal their hideout to the patrols of Philistines roaming the countryside looking for these three daring invaders. When they returned to David they were breathless, both from the arduous journey and from the excitement. "My lord, the king," Jashobean said. "Eleazar, Shammah and I overheard you asking for a drink from the well at Bethlehem near the gate. Have we got a surprise for you! In this cruse is fresh water from the well of your youth."

129

They handed the cruse to David joyfully. He had a puzzled look on his face, as if to say, "How did they do that? Why did they do that? They risked their lives for me."

By this time a crowd had gathered around David. They could sense the excitement. Then David did the most unexpected thing. He held the cruse of pristine water high above his head and poured it out on the ground. Jashobeam was speechless, but not David. The man after God's own heart said, "Far be it from me, O my God, that I should do this! Shall I drink the blood of these men who have put their lives in jeopardy? For at the risk of their lives they brought it" (v. 19).

Abed interrupted his uncle. "Wait a minute. Do you mean that after Jashobeam and the others risked their lives for David, he didn't even drink the water? What a waste!"

"No, Abed," Nibshan replied. "Whatever we offer to God is never a waste. The greater the value, the greater the offering. David treasured the water in that cruse. That's why instead of drinking it to his own enjoyment, he offered it to God in thanksgiving for the daring service of the three."

Finding Significance in Service

Seeing the perfect opportunity to teach Abed a valuable lesson, Nibshan seized it. He explained to his nephew why Jashobeam wrote in the scroll, "Today I served my master well. Today he honored me by honoring God. I risked my life for David, and he expressed his devotion to God by giving the fruit of my labors to Him."

We all serve others. Sometimes it's our parents, sometimes our spouses, sometimes our employers, sometimes our churches. Christians are in the service business because we are in the salvation business. The real question is, How do we find significance in service when we are working for others? Jashobeam knew the answer.

The chief of all became the servant to one, the one he loved—David. He would have done anything for David. Serving him was the joy of Jashobeam's heart. What he did in risking his life for David, he did for the one he knew was the man after God's own heart. It's easy to work for those who work for God. Jashobeam brought the cruse of fresh water to David, but there was no lasting disappointment when David poured it out as a sacrifice to God. David's sacrifice was ultimately Jashobeam's sacrifice. David honored Jashobeam in honoring God.

Sometimes it seems as if we work hard and others get all the attention. We do our job day after day and everyone thinks our boss is brilliant because his division gets so much done. We prepare well and teach faithfully our Sunday school class, and people all over town talk about what a great job our pastor is doing in educating his church. There's a lesson from Jashobeam we all must learn. When those we honor in turn honor God, we honor God too. When those we serve in turn serve God, we serve God too.

Jashobeam could thank God for David and even for David pouring out the cruse of water. David did it not out of ingratitude toward Jashobeam, but in thankfulness for him. David honored God with his sacrifice, but he acknowledged that the real sacrifice that honored God was Jashobeam's.

Nibshan rolled up the scroll, handed it to Abed and said, "Now, if you have learned the lesson of Jashobeam, take the scroll to the hills and put it back where you found it. There will be other young shepherds in years to come who need to learn this lesson too."

But Abed objected, "Uncle, can't I keep it? I found it." Nibshan smiled knowingly and replied, "Yes, Abed, you did find it, but others will need to find it as well. After all, your father and I put it back after we found it nearly forty years ago. We knew someday one of your brothers or you would be tending the sheep in those hills and you would need to be encouraged by one of God's little people."

The secret to serving others is to know that ultimately you are serving God. Do your work for others as if you were doing it for God, and you will be doing it for God. You may not be familiar with Jashobeam's name, but who can forget the risk he took to serve David? God uses ordinary people, little people, people like Jashobeam, people just like you and me. Serve well and let Him turn your ordinary service into extraordinary honor.

JOANNA

Name:	**Joanna**
Nationality:	Jewess
Era:	Circa A.D. 30
Location:	Jerusalem
Reference:	Luke 8:2-3; 23:55-56; 24:1,10

Most Memorable Accomplishment:

In the Roman era, which was a hard and repressive time, women were rarely mentioned with their husbands, let alone without them. Still, some women are referred to by name in the New Testament because of their contribution or character. Joanna was such a woman. To her husband, Chuza, King Herod Antipas had committed the education of household children. This put Joanna in a position of higher esteem than one would ordinarily expect. But Joanna's claim to fame was not her husband but her own faithfulness to her Master. Healed of a disease by Jesus, she followed Him constantly from Galilee to Judea for the rest of His earthly life. She ministered to His needs while He lived and after He died. Though she lived in Herod's court, she never forgot who was really the King of the Jews.

CHAPTER 13

Joanna

A Believer in King Herod's Court

This is my private journal. I'm letting you read it because I want you to know my Savior as I know Him. He is so precious to me; He has done so much for me. I haven't shared my journal with anyone before, but maybe it will encourage you. I am Joanna, and I traveled with Jesus and the others for several years.

I should tell you that He's gone now. They came one night to the garden where the olive groves grow and rudely took Him to Caiaphas and then to Pilate. He was condemned to die, and on that awful day, that absolutely horrible day, they crucified Him. I was there; I saw it happen. I'll never forget it. And then a couple days later, His tomb was empty. He is alive! I know, I couldn't believe it at first either, but I saw Him. I saw Him standing there as alive as you and I are. Jesus is alive! He has risen from the dead!

He's gone back to the Father now, where He came from. It was quite a sight, Jesus being taken up into the clouds. Then there were the angels promising He would return. I have to tell you, it made quite an impression on all of us.

But I'm getting ahead of myself. Let me tell you about me, about how I came to know Him.

I am a devout Jewess. You probably guessed that from my name. It means, "Jehovah has been gracious," and He has been so gracious to me. I have a wonderful husband, a wonderful life and oh, yes, did I mention I have a wonderful Savior?

Herod's Household

My husband's name is Chuza. That's not a very common name. It's a family name actually. Chuza and I have been married for many years. God gave us a delightful family, but the nest is empty now. The children are all grown and gone; they have lives of their own.

Chuza has quite a responsible position. He is the steward for Herod Antipas, the king. In case you don't know, let me tell you what my husband does. There are two kinds of stewards in Roman households. One manages the affairs of the house—he orders the supplies, does the accounting, that sort of thing. That's a good job, but Chuza's job is even better.

Chuza is a teacher; that's the other kind of steward. He is a tutor for the palace children. He is one of many who are responsible for educating the children of the palace staff. The vizier's children are in Chuza's classes, and so are the children of Herod's director of public works and the daughter of the finance minister. Chuza tutors the children of those closest to Herod. And everybody knows Chuza. He is such a good teacher. He helps shape the lives of the future leaders of the Roman Empire.

We live in an apartment adjacent to the palace. It's not large, but with the children gone now, it's more than adequate. Every day I mingle with the other wives and employees of the palace. We talk and we talk. We discuss everything from the hot weather to what Antipas will be up to next. I very much enjoy having this free access to the palace. In fact, it used to be the most significant thing in my life. I say "used to be" because now that I have met Jesus, nothing or no one could ever compare to Him in significance.

Jesus Healed Me

I first met Jesus several years ago. My friend Mary, from Magdala, introduced me to him. Mary was quite a character. She was wild and reckless as a young girl. I didn't know her then; I don't think I would have liked her then. If her parents said, "Don't do it," Mary did it. If someone said, "Mary don't say that," Mary said it.

Mary Magdalene had been having trouble with demons. She got involved in things she shouldn't have and seven demons came into her body and took over. This went on for a long time. Mary was miserable. Who wouldn't be? Her body was host to seven evil spirits who caused her nothing but anguish.

One day Jesus of Nazareth was walking along the shore of the Sea of Galilee. We call it Kinnereth. Mary lived near there in Magdala, on the western shore of the lake. She was wild and crude. Jesus was kind and gentle. It was like the darkness coming face-to-face with the light. Jesus looked at Mary, had compassion for her, and with power and great authority commanded the seven spirits to leave her. Instantly they were gone. I mean instantly! The Light of the World pierced the darkness of the world and Mary's life was changed forever. She had faith in Jesus and trusted Him as her Savior and Lord.

After Mary and I became friends, she knew I was troubled myself. I, too, felt the oppression of demonic spirits. It was driving me crazy. And to make matters worse, my health wasn't good. I was sick all the time and didn't know what to do. Mary said, "Jesus will know what to do. Look what He did for me. If Jesus can change my life and heal me, He can do the same for you."

She was right. I met Jesus one day. He laid His hand on my shoulder and prayed for me. And I tell you, since that moment my health has been great and I haven't felt even one evil spirit in me. I'm a new woman, thanks to Jesus. How grateful I am to Mary for introducing me to Him. Now I introduce Him to others who need Him just like I did.

Good Friends of Mine

Mary Magdalene is my good friend, maybe my best friend. We do everything together. Chuza doesn't mind. He knows there's been a change in my life since I met Mary, and now he knows why. You see, one time my husband asked me, "Joanna, you seem so different. What's wrong with you?" I explained, "Oh, my dear Chuza, nothing is wrong with me. Now that I've met Jesus, everything is right with me."

That day I had the opportunity to tell my loving husband how Jesus healed me from my sickness, cleansed me from the demons and, most important of all, told me how to have life everlasting. I told Chuza about my love for Jesus as my Messiah and he said that's what he was looking for too. Now Chuza has expressed his faith in our Messiah and our life together has never been sweeter.

Chuza has been so kind. Mary told me that Jesus and His disciples needed help with the normal needs of people who travel around the country and that she had volunteered to help. She wanted to know if I could help too. I asked Chuza about it and he agreed. It was something I could do and should do. I'd only be away from home when Jesus was traveling out of Jerusalem. I'd be home every night when the Master was in town. Chuza said, "I have my children to teach; you have our Master to serve. You need to do it." He is so considerate.

There were more than just Mary Magdalene and myself who helped. Susanna also joined us. She was a widow and free to travel. A little older than Mary and me, Susanna had a special gift of wisdom. She always knew just what to do. She loves Jesus so much. I have learned a great deal from her, and I appreciate her so deeply.

And it was good to have the other Mary travel with us too. She was the mother of "Little James," as we called him. He is James the Less, who was one of Jesus' disciples. We used to give these pet names to each other because there were so many men named James or Simon or Joseph, and so many women named Mary or Anna or Elizabeth.

There were dozens more who helped, of course. It was a big job. We all came from very different backgrounds. Some were older, some were younger, some of us were middle-aged. Now that I think of it, we women were about as diverse as Jesus' disciples—and everybody talked about how different they were. But we all had one thing in common. We were completely devoted to Jesus. We were willing to travel the dusty trails of Galilee and the back roads of the Jordan Valley, or we would climb the hills to Jerusalem if He was willing. And He always seemed to be so willing to go where people needed Him. It was a joy to hear Him teach.

Doing What I Can

When Mary first asked me to help out and Chuza gave me his blessing, I wondered what I could do. Chuza is the gifted one in our family. He teaches in a way that everyone can understand. I can't do that. What could I do? Mary made it so simple for me. She said, "Do what you can. That's all that Jesus asks."

Another friend of mine named Mary learned that too. She lived in Bethany and was the sister of Martha and Lazarus. When she anointed Jesus' head with oil just before they took Him away to crucify Him, Judas (God forgive him) and some of the others complained. They criticized Mary for wasting the oil; it could have been sold and the money given to the poor, they said. But Jesus defended Mary. He said, "Let her alone. Why do you trouble her? She has done what she could."

Doing what I can, if it's done for my Master, is better than just dreaming about doing great things and accomplishing nothing. I'm never going to walk on water, as Jesus did. I'm never going to preach, as Peter does. I'm not able to do those things. But do you know what? I make a mean falafel. You should taste my lentil soup. Jesus used to say my bread was as good as His mother used to make in Nazareth. I can cook, and that's what I did for Jesus and His disciples. They had to eat, too, you know. Mary the mother of James and I used to do most of the cooking.

We also washed clothes in the Jordan River and laid them out on the rocks to dry in the sun. Those roads get pretty dusty during the summer and muddy in the winter. It seemed like a never-ending job keeping robes cleaned and clothes fresh. We used to mix a little olive oil with our soap fat when we washed the disciples' robes. It kept them soft and sweet-smelling.

God had perfected my homemaking skills while the children were still at home. Maybe that's why He gave me a family, so I would have the right tools to serve my Savior. Isn't it wonderful how God had this all figured out!

I've Got Big News

You may remember that earlier I mentioned that I was present when they crucified my Lord. We were all so scared. Most of us hid in the shadows or stood at the edge of the crowd. We were in shock. We didn't know what was happening.

I saw Him carry His cross to the place where the Romans punish people. So many had died at "the Skull" before, but never anyone like Jesus. The soldiers nailed Him to the cross and raised it up. It slid into the hole at the base with a thud. I remember wincing when I saw the pain on Jesus' face. He hung on that cross throughout the morning. It seemed like forever. Later in the day, when He died, I heard Him shout something. There was a definite hint of victory in His voice. It was all over. There was a sense of accomplishment that I don't yet fully understand. But it was there. Mark my word, the victory was there!

Some of the men took Jesus' body down from the cross before sunset and buried it in a nearby tomb. Mary and I watched where they took Him because no one had prepared His body for burial. That was something else we could do.

Very early in the morning, before dawn on the first day of the week, Mary Magdalene, Mary the mother of James, some of the other women and I met at the tomb. Our Savior had been so kind to all of us, and we wanted to give Him a proper burial. I brought some sweet spice and so did the others. We Jews don't embalm a dead body like the Egyptians do; we perfume it and wrap it in cloth for burial. That's what the others and I came to do that morning.

When we arrived at the tomb we got the shock of our lives. The stone the Roman soldiers had rolled over the opening of the sepulcher was moved. You could see right into the rock-cut tomb. We didn't know who moved the huge stone, but we were grateful. I don't think all of us together would have had the strength to move it.

We went into the sepulcher to do our work, but to our amazement, Jesus' body was gone! Not misplaced or moved—it was gone! And off to the side were two angels who told us not to be afraid. We still shook a little. They said Jesus was not there;

He had risen from the dead just as He said He would. Now that I think back on the days leading up to His crucifixion, I do remember Him saying something about rising from the dead. I should have listened more carefully.

Well, we couldn't keep news like this to ourselves. We had to tell someone, but whom? "Peter," someone said, "we must tell Peter." Another chimed in, "And John too." We had to run as fast as our aging legs could carry us to tell the eleven the good news. Jesus is alive!

At first they didn't believe us. It was as if they were half asleep. Well, it was still early in the morning. Maybe some of them were still sleepy. But soon Peter and John were out the door like a flash and off to the tomb to see for themselves.

I have often though how good God was to the other ladies and myself. Just think. We were the first ones to see the empty tomb. We were the first ones to know Jesus had risen from the dead. We were the first ones to tell the story that will be told millions of times again around the world. I just know it will. We women, ordinary women, were the first ones to know that Jesus is alive. Was God rewarding us for things others would not?

Don't look for my name written in the list of the important people who followed Jesus. I'm not Peter or James. I'm not even like my friend Mary Magdalene. I'm just a housewife who did what she could for the Lord Jesus.

So what can you do for the Master? What are the tasks you can accomplish that will speed the message on its way that Jesus is alive? Cooking, cleaning, washing, serving—these things aren't very glamorous, but even unglamorous things have to get done. If you don't do them, who will?

You may be like me. I'm one of God's little people. Not many people will recognize my name, but Jesus does. He knows who I am and what I've done.

What does Jesus expect from you? Just do what you can. That's all Jesus asks. When you do what you can, faithfully and completely for His glory, you'll discover what a big God can do with what we little people do for Him. And one day, even we little people will hear a booming "Well done!" from the only One who matters.

If I had the choice of being a big name who does things that don't matter or being a little name who does things that do, you know which I'd take. Jesus just wants us to make ourselves available to Him. He'll find something for us to do, and He'll make it worthwhile.

I thank God for people like James and Peter and John. God has called them to a great work. But God has called me to a great work too. If I didn't do it, it wouldn't get done. God is a big God, but He uses little people—people just like you and me.

Conclusion

Does anybody know who you are? Is recognition of your work conspicuously absent from the church bulletin week after week? Instead of being listed in *Who's Who*, is your name listed in *Who's That?*

We have come to believe in society today that if your name makes the headlines, if you get your picture in the paper, if you're seen on television or heard on radio, somehow you're important. And if no one recognizes your name, you're just one of those nondescript little people who never contributes anything.

As this book has demonstrated, however, some of God's greatest heroes, the people who have accomplished the greatest exploits for Him, are barely known to us. You likely do not recognize Sherebiah the temple servant. How about Tychicus the amanuensis? Or Shemaiah the prophet? Not familiar with them? They're all Bible heroes. They all distinguished themselves in service to God. They have great stories that could just as easily have been told in this book as well.

Let's face it. People like Ittai the Gittite, Barzillai, Jahaziel or Joanna are not household names. They're not the kind of people who get their name in lights or their picture in the paper. They're just ordinary people through whom God did extraordinary things.

Maybe you're one of God's little people. Even those in your church don't know your name. But you have a job to do for God and that makes you significant. God has a service in mind for each of us, and He has perfectly equipped us to do whatever He

145

has in mind. You can be a champion for God. Just give yourself totally to Him for whatever task needs to be done and let Him do extraordinary things through you.

I pray that reading about some of God's little people in this book has encouraged you. After all, it's not just the people whose names are in lights who are important to God. You are important to Him too. You have a big God who is in the habit of using little people to do big things. Take heart. You don't have to be famous to be significant in God's sight. He delights in using little people— people just like you and me.